A-Z TAUNTON

CONTE

| Key to Map Pages | 2-3 |
| Map Pages | 4-31 |

REFERE

Motorway	M5	Car Park Selected	P
A Road	A38	Church or Chapel	†
B Road	B3170	Fire Station	■
Dual Carriageway		Hospital	H
One-way Street Traffic flow on A roads is indicated by a heavy line on the drivers' left.	→	House Numbers A & B Roads only	218 17
Restricted Access		Information Centre	i
Pedestrianized Road		National Grid Reference	320
Track & Footpath		Police Station	▲
Residential Walkway		Post Office	★
Railway	Level Crossing / Tunnel / Heritage Station / Station	Toilet with facilities for the disabled	▽ ♿
Built-up Area	NEW ST.	Educational Establishment	
Posttown Boundary		Hospital or Hospice	
Postcode Boundary		Industrial Building	
		Leisure or Recreational Facility	
		Place of Interest	
Map Continuation	12	Public Building	
		Shopping Centre or Market	
		Other Selected Buildings	

Scale

1:15,840

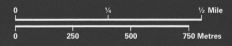

4 inches (10.16 cm) to 1 mile
6.31 cm to 1km

Copyright of Geographers' A-Z Map Company Ltd.

Head Office :
Fairfield Road, Borough Green, Sevenoaks, Kent TN15 8PP
Telephone: 01732 781000
www.a-zmaps.co.uk

Ordnance Survey® This product includes mapping data licensed from Ordnance Survey with the permission of the Controller of Her Majesty's Stationery Office.
© Crown Copyright 2004. Licence number 100017302

Copyright © Geographers' A-Z Map Co. Ltd. 2004   EDITION 1 2002   EDITION 1a 2004 (Part Revision)

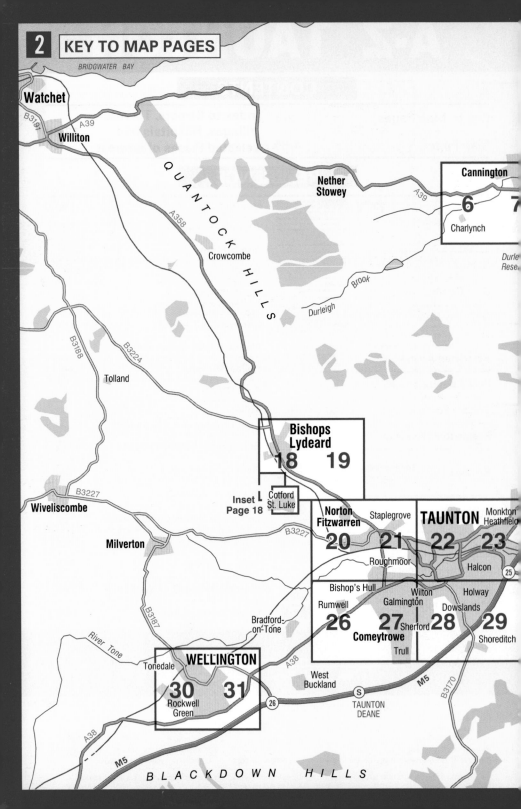

BRIDGWATER BAY

Watchet

B3191

A39

Williton

Q U A N T O C K

A358

Nether
Stowey

A39

Cannington

6 **7**

Charlynch

Crowcombe

H I L L S

Durle
Rese

Brook

Durleigh

B3188

B3224

Tolland

Bishops
Lydeard

18 **19**

B3227

Wiveliscombe

Inset
Page 18

Cotford
St. Luke

Norton
Fitzwarren

Staplegrove

TAUNTON

Monkton
Heathfield

Milverton

B3227

20 **21** **22** **23**

Roughmoor

Halcon

25

B3187

Bishop's Hull

Wilton

Holway

River Tone

Rumwell

Galmington

Dowslands

Bradford-
on-Tone

26 **27** **28** **29**

Sherford

Shoreditch

Comeytrowe

Trull

WELLINGTON

A38

Tonedale

30 **31**

West
Buckland

M5

B3170

Rockwell
Green

26

S

TAUNTON
DEANE

A38

M5

B L A C K D O W N   H I L L S

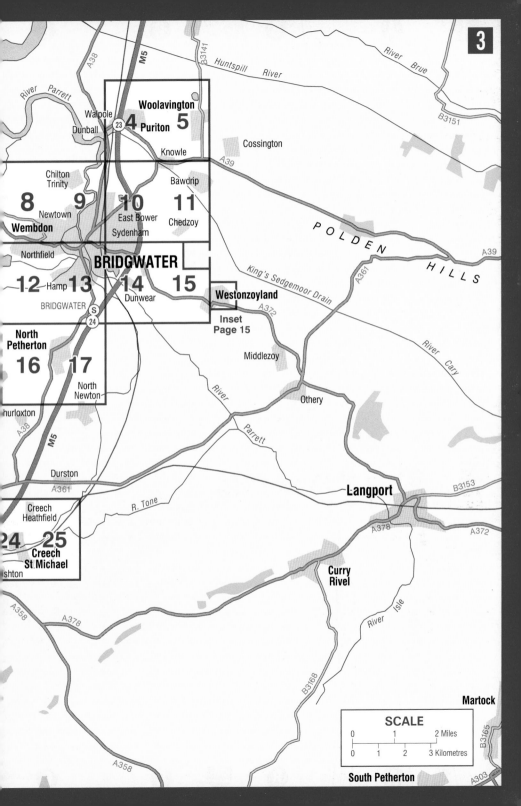

3

River Brue

Huntspill River

River Parrett

A38

M5

B3141

B3151

Woolavington

Walpole
Dunball
4 Puriton **5**

Knowle

Cossington

A39

POLDEN

HILLS

A39

Chilton
Trinity

Bawdrip

8 Newtown **9** **10** East Bower **11**

Wembdon

Sydenham
BRIDGEWATER

Chedzoy

Northfield

A361

A39

12 Hamp **13** **14** Dunwear **15**

BRIDGWATER

King's Sedgemoor Drain

Westonzoyland

A372

Inset
Page 15

North
Petherton

16 **17**

Middlezoy

River Cary

North
Newton

Othery

hurloxton

River

A38

M5

Parrett

Durston
A361

Langport

B3153

R. Tone

A378

A372

24 **25**
Creech
St. Michael

Creech
Heathfield

Curry
Rivel

shton

River Isle

A358

A378

Martock

A358

B3168

B3165

A303

SCALE

0   1   2 Miles

0   1   2   3 Kilometres

South Petherton

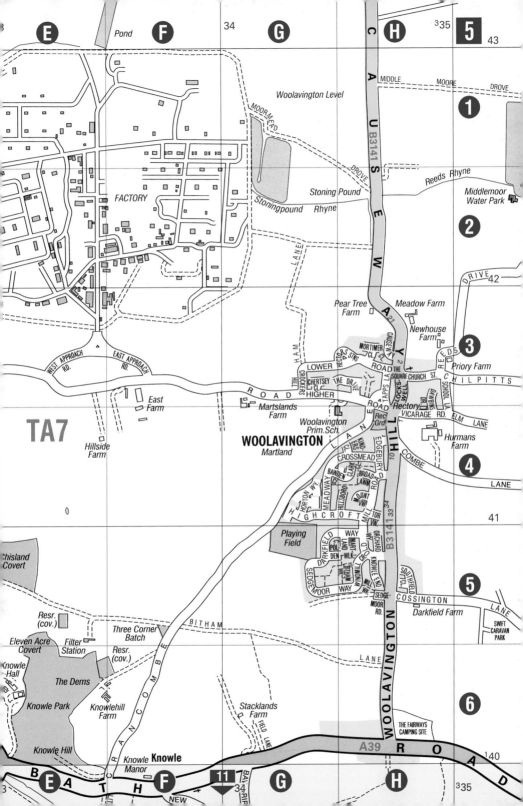

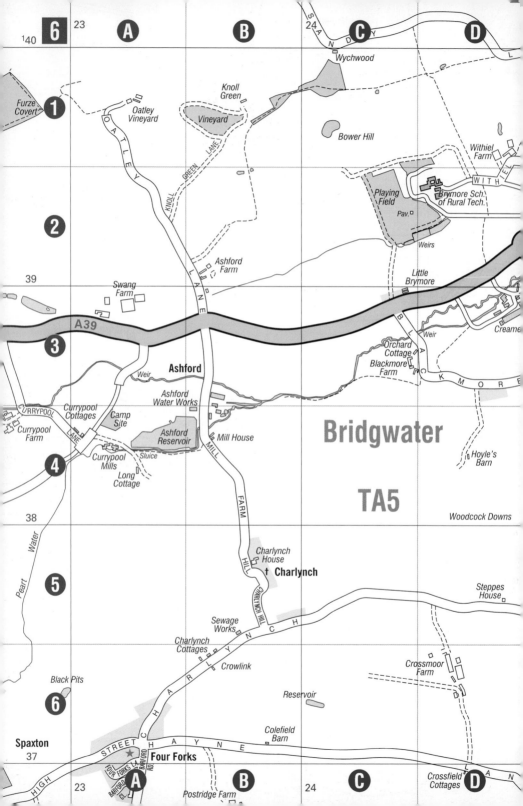

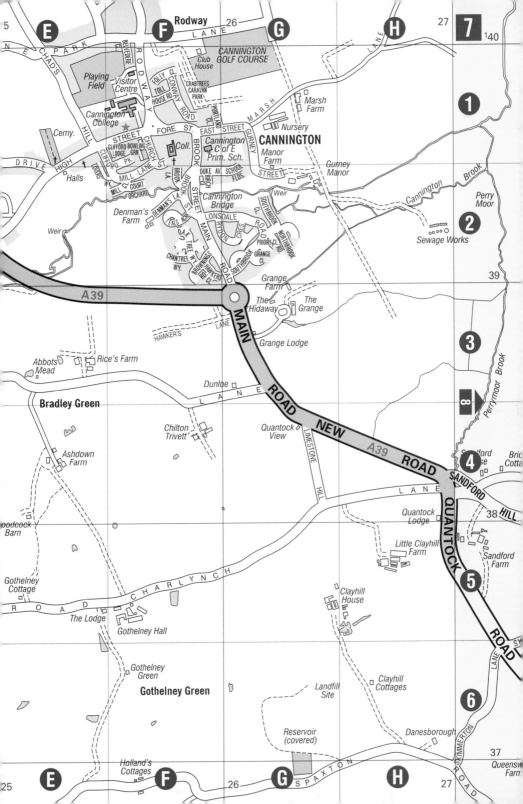

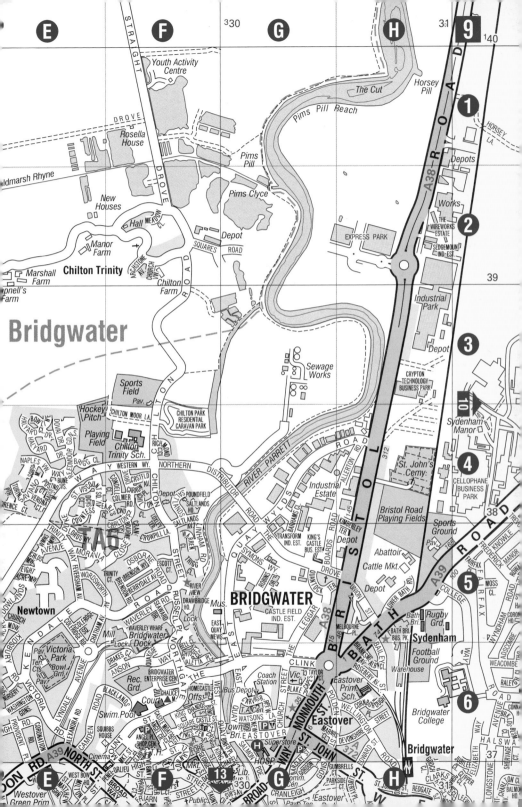

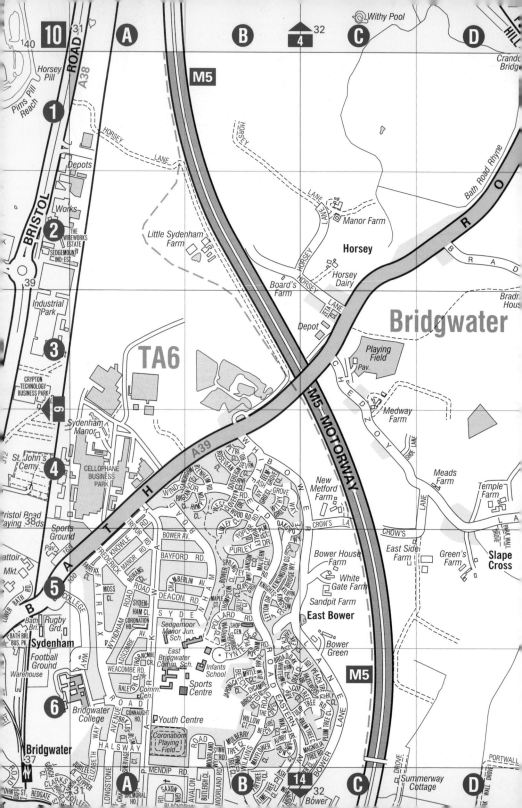

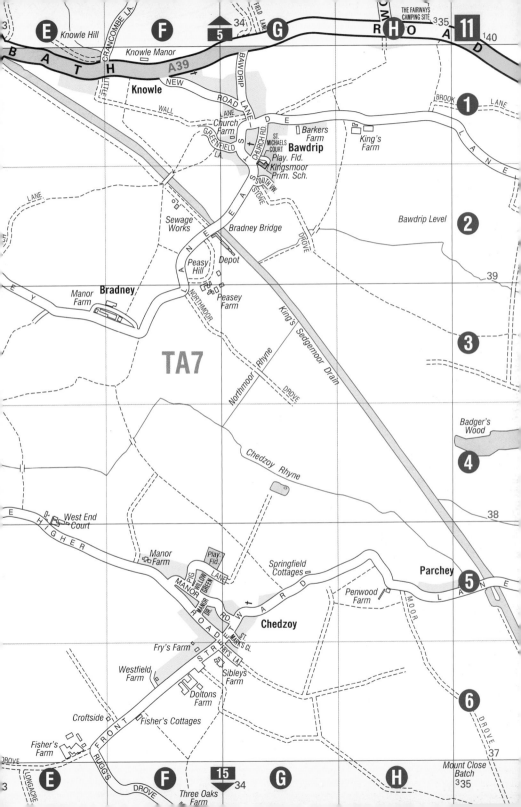

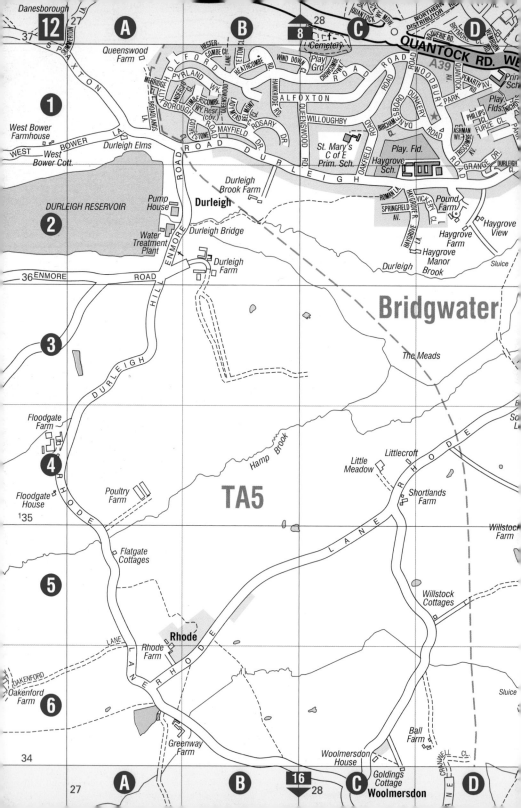

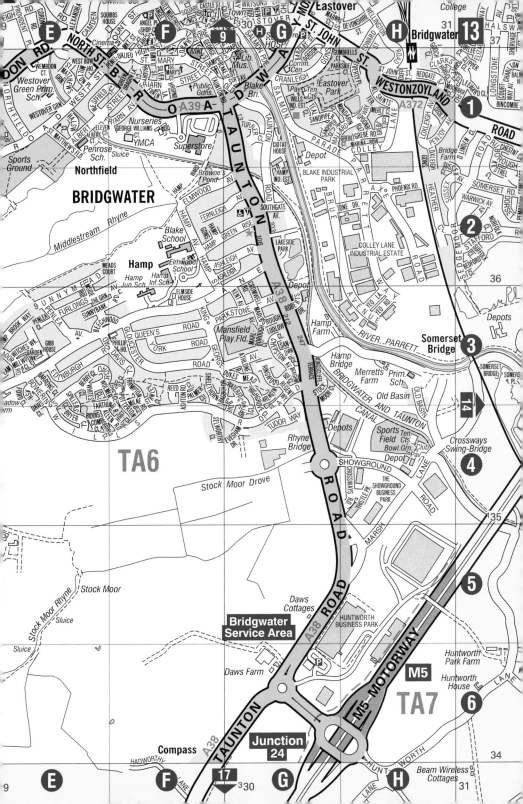

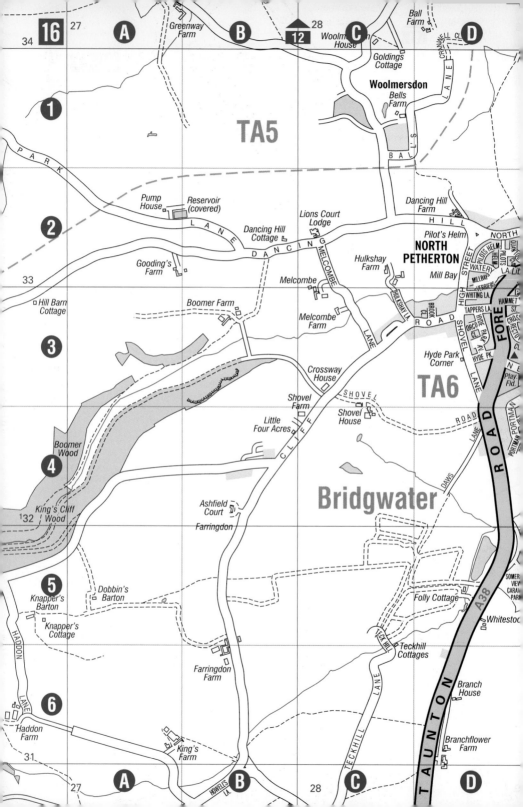

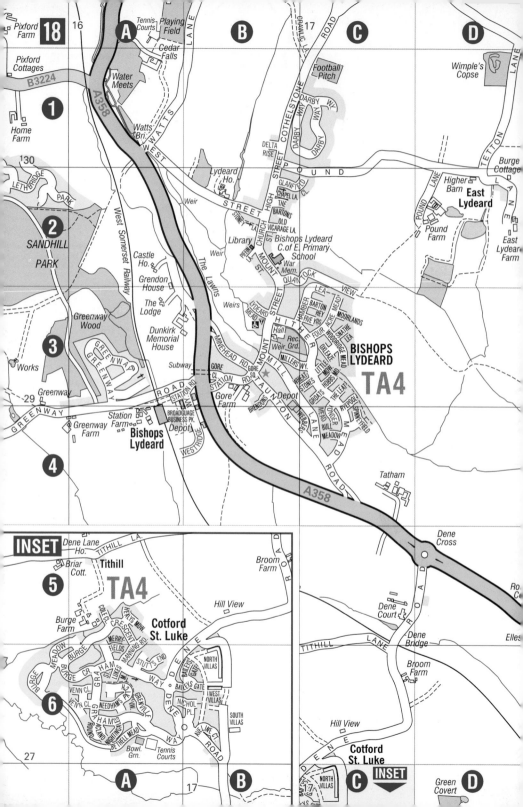

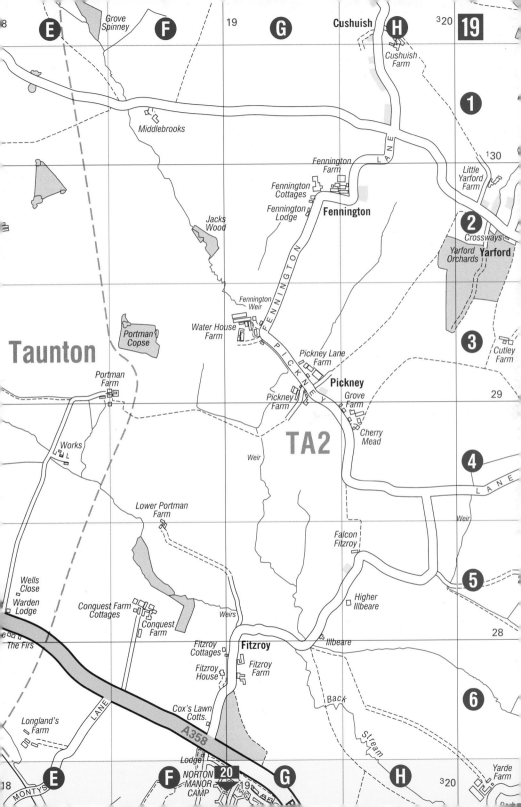

E Grove Spinney F 19 G Cushuish H 320 **19**

Cushuish Farm

1

Middlebrooks

130

Jacks Wood

Fennington Farm

Fennington Cottages

Little Yarford Farm

Fennington Lodge **Fennington**

2

Crossways

Yarford Orchards **Yarford**

Taunton

Fennington Weir

Portman Copse

Water House Farm

Fennington

Pickney Lane Farm

3

Cutley Farm

Portman Farm

PICKNEY

Pickney

29

Pickney Farm

Grove Farm

TA2

Cherry Mead

Works L

Weir

4

LANE

Weir

Lower Portman Farm

Falcon Fitzroy

Wells Close

Warden Lodge

5

Conquest Farm Cottages

Higher Illbeare

28

Conquest Farm

Weirs

The Firs

Fitzroy Cottages **Fitzroy**

Illbeare

Fitzroy House

Fitzroy Farm

Back

6

Cox's Lawn Cotts.

Longland's Farm

Stream

Lodge

Yarde Farm

E **20** F **NORTON MANOR CAMP** 19 G H 320

18 MONTYS A358

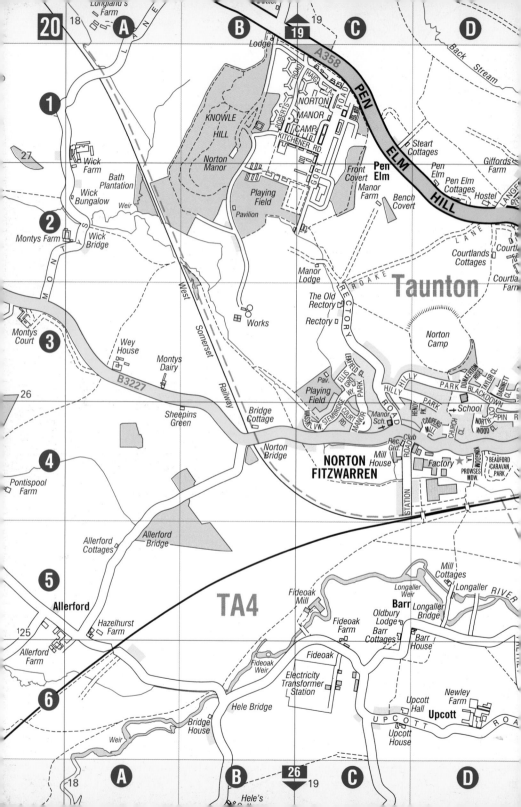

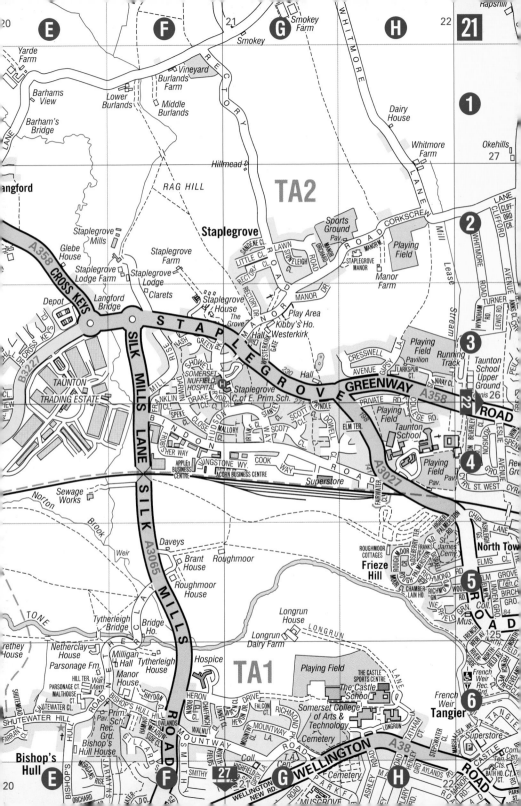

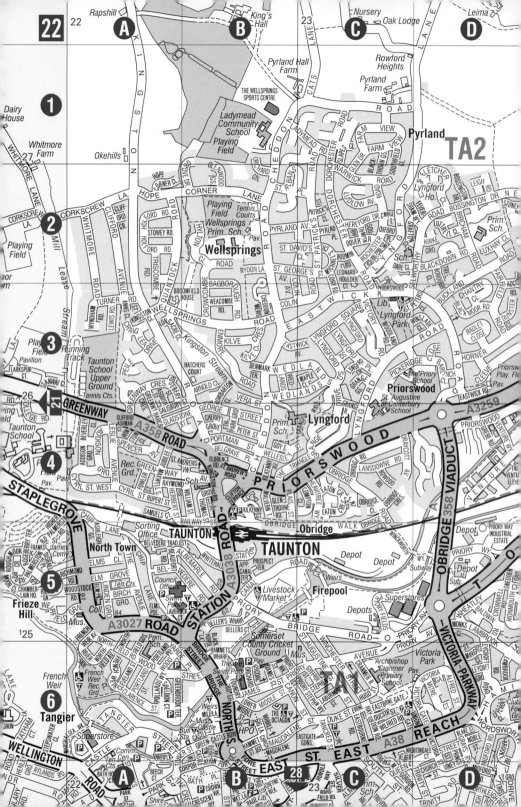

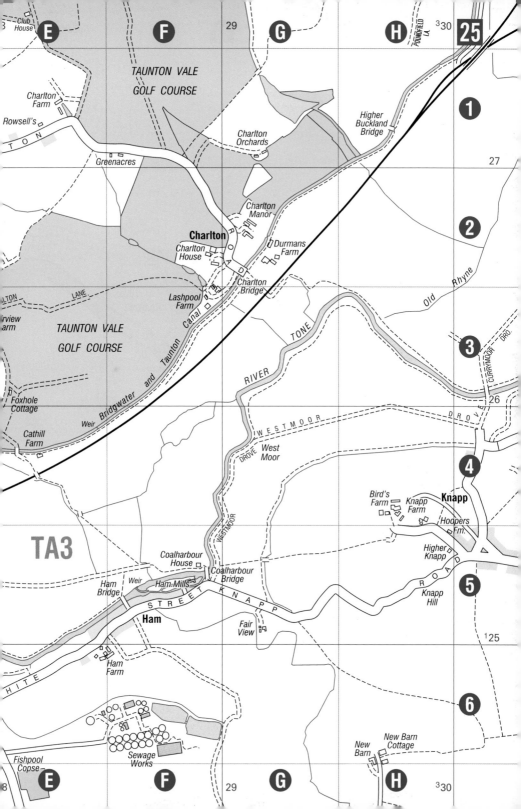

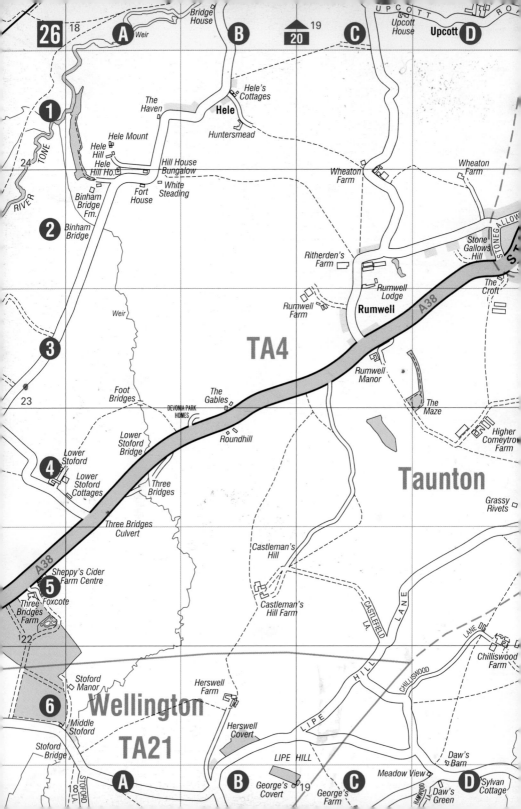

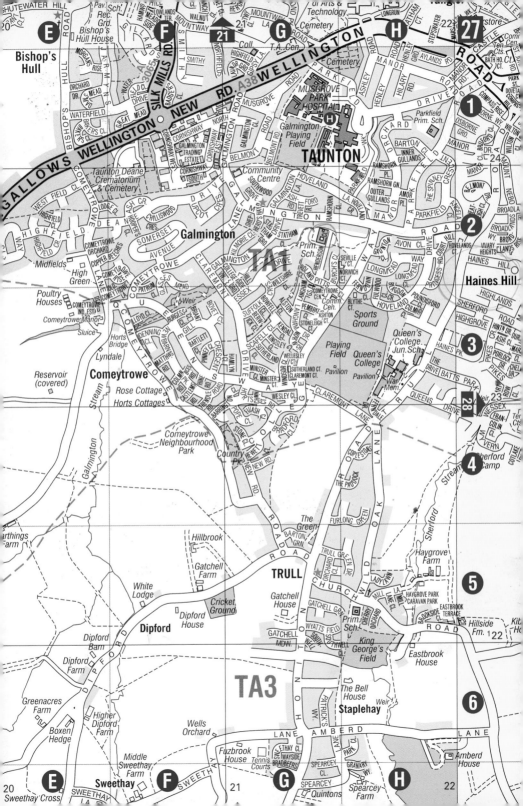

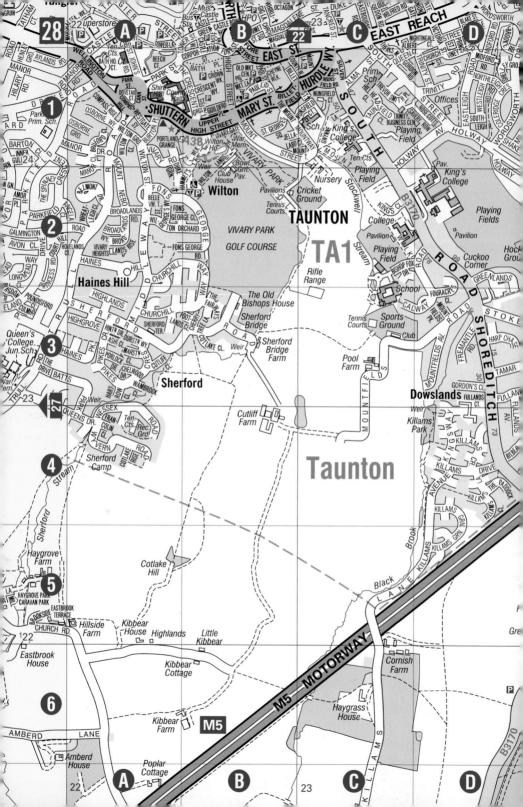

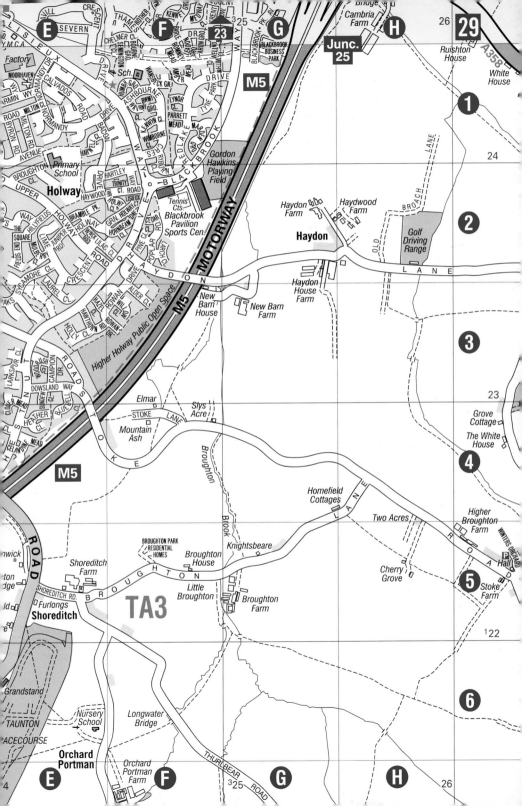

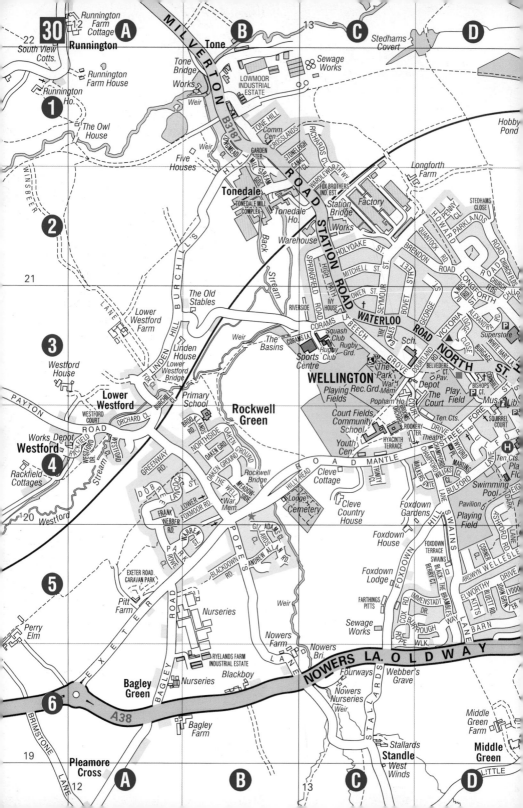

INDEX

Including Streets, Places & Areas, Hospitals & Hospices, Industrial Estates,
Selected Flats & Walkways and Selected Places of Interest.

HOW TO USE THIS INDEX

1. Each street name is followed by its Postal District and then by its Locality abbreviation(s) and then by its map reference;
e.g. **Acacia Gdns.** TA2: B'pool ....3G **23** is in the Taunton 2 Postal District and the Bathpool Locality and is to be found in square 3G on page **23**.
The page number is shown in bold type.

2. A strict alphabetical order is followed in which Av., Rd., St., etc. (though abbreviated) are read in full and as part of the street name;
e.g. **Black Horse La.** appears after **Blackdown Vw.** but before **Blacklands**.

3. Streets and a selection of flats and walkways too small to be shown on the maps, appear in the index with the thoroughfare to which it is connected
shown in brackets; e.g. **Admirals Ct.** TA6: B'wtr....6F **9** (off Quayside)

4. Places and areas are shown in the index in blue type and the map reference is to the actual map square in which the town centre or area is located and
not to the place name shown on the map; e.g. **Bishops Lydeard** 3B **18**

5. An example of a selected place of interest is Admiral Blake Mus. 1G **13**

6. An example of a hospital or hospice is BRIDGWATER COMMUNITY HOSPITAL 6G **9**

GENERAL ABBREVIATIONS

& : And	**E.** : East	**Lwr.** : Lower	**St** : Saint
App. : Approach	**Ent.** : Enterprise	**Mnr.** : Manor	**Shop.** : Shopping
Av. : Avenue	**Est.** : Estate	**Mkt.** : Market	**Sq.** : Square
Bldgs. : Buildings	**Fld.** : Field	**Mdw.** : Meadow	**Sth.** : South
Bri. : Bridge	**Flds.** : Fields	**M.** : Mews	**St.** : Street
Bus. : Business	**Gdns.** : Gardens	**Mus.** : Museum	**Ter.** : Terrace
Cvn. : Caravan	**Ga.** : Gate	**Nth.** : North	**Trad.** : Trading
Cen. : Centre	**Grn.** : Green	**Pde.** : Parade	**Up.** : Upper
Circ. : Circle	**Gro.** : Grove	**Pk.** : Park	**Vw.** : View
Cl. : Close	**Ho.** : House	**Pas.** : Passage	**Vs.** : Villas
Cotts. : Cottages	**Ind.** : Industrial	**Pl.** : Place	**Vis.** : Visitors
Ct. : Court	**Info.** : Information	**Res.** : Residential	**Wlk.** : Walk
Cres. : Crescent	**La.** : Lane	**Ri.** : Rise	**W.** : West
Dr. : Drive	**Lit.** : Little	**Rd.** : Road	

LOCALITY ABBREVIATIONS

B Grn : **Bagley Green**	Creech M : **Creech St Michael**	Nails : **Nailsbourne**	Spax : **Spaxton**
B'pool : **Bathpool**	D'ball : **Dunball**	N Curry : **North Curry**	Staple : **Staplegrove**
B'drip : **Bawdrip**	Durl : **Durleigh**	N New : **North Newton**	Stoke M : **Stoke St Mary**
Bish H : **Bishop's Hull**	Durs : **Durston**	N Peth : **North Petherton**	Taun : **Taunton**
Bish L : **Bishops Lydeard**	D'wear : **Dunwear**	Nort F : **Norton Fitzwarren**	Thurl : **Thurlbear**
B'wtr : **Bridgwater**	E Bwr : **East Bower**	P'lett : **Pawlett**	Thurlo : **Thurloxton**
Cann : **Cannington**	Goat : **Goathurst**	Poole : **Poole**	Tone : **Tonedale**
Charl : **Charlynch**	Ham : **Ham**	P'ton : **Puriton**	Trull : **Trull**
Ched F : **Cheddon Fitzpaine**	H'don : **Haydon**	Rhode : **Rhode**	Well : **Wellington**
C'zoy : **Chedzoy**	H'lade : **Henlade**	R Grn : **Rockwell Green**	Wemb : **Wembdon**
C'ston : **Chelston**	H'sey : **Horsey**	R'moor : **Roughmoor**	W Buck : **West Buckland**
Chil T : **Chilton Trinity**	Hunt : **Huntworth**	Ruish : **Ruishton**	West : **Westford**
Comey : **Comeytrowe**	King M : **Kingston St Mary**	R'ton : **Runnington**	W Monk : **West Monkton**
Coss : **Cossington**	Kwle : **Knowle**	R'well : **Runwell**	W'land : **Westonzoyland**
Cott L : **Cotford St Luke**	Lang : **Langaller**	Samp A : **Sampford Arundel**	Wlvgtn : **Woolavington**
Creech H : **Creech Heathfield**	Monk H : **Monkton Heathfield**	Shore : **Shoreditch**	Wool : **Woolmersdon**

INDEX

A

Acacia Gdns. TA2: B'pool 3G **23**
Acland Round TA4: Cotf L......6A **18**
Acorn Bus. Cen. TA2: Taun ...4G **21**
Adcombe Rd. TA2: Taun 2D **22**
Addison Gro. TA2: Taun 4A **22**
Admiral Blake Mus. 1G **13**
Admirals Ct. TA6: B'wtr........6F **9**
         (off Quayside)
Admiralty Way TA1: Taun.......4E **23**
Adscombe Av. TA6: B'wtr......6A **10**
Albemarle Cen. TA1: Taun 5B **22**
      (off Albemarle Rd.)
Albemarle Rd. TA1: Taun......5B **22**
Albert Ct. TA1: Taun 6C **22**
  TA6: B'wtr......................1E **13**
Albert St. TA6: B'wtr............1E **13**
Albion Cl. TA6: B'wtr............6H **9**
Alder Cl. TA1: Taun..............3F **29**
  TA6: N Peth....................3E **17**
Alderney Rd. TA6: B'wtr.......2A **14**

Alexander Cl.
  TA3: Creech M................3C **24**
Alexandra Rd. TA6: B'wtr.......6E **9**
  TA21: Well.....................3D **30**
Alexevia Cvn. Pk.
  TA3: Ruish.....................6B **24**
Alfoxton Rd. TA6: B'wtr.......1B **12**
Alfred St. TA1: Taun............6D **22**
Allen Rd. TA6: B'wtr............4E **13**
Allerford 5A **20**
Allerton Rd. TA6: B'wtr........4H **9**
Allington Cl. TA1: Taun........6G **23**
All Saints' Ter. TA6: B'wtr....1H **13**
Alma St. TA1: Taun 1C **28**
Almond Tree Cl.
  TA6: B'wtr......................1B **14**
Alston Cl. TA1: Taun............3G **27**
Amberd La. TA3: Trull..........6G **27**
Amber Mead TA1: Taun 1F **29**
Amor Pl. TA1: Taun..............2H **27**
Andersfield Cl. TA6: B'wtr 1A **12**
Andrew Allan Rd.
  TA21: R Grn...................5B **30**

Angela Cl. TA1: Taun 2H **27**
Angel Cres. TA6: B'wtr.........6F **9**
Angel Pl. Shop. Cen.
  TA6: B'wtr......................6F **9**
Anson Way TA6: B'wtr 6F **9**
Apple Bus. Cen.
  TA1: Taun.......................4F **21**
Apple Tree Cl. TA6: B'wtr......1B **14**
Apricot Tree Cl.
  TA6: B'wtr......................6B **10**
Archstone Av. TA5: Chil T 2F **9**
Ardwyn TA21: Well...............5D **30**
Arlington Cl. TA6: B'wtr 3G **13**
Arnold Cl. TA2: Taun 3B **22**
Arundells Way
  TA3: Creech M................4B **24**
Arun Gro. TA1: Taun 1F **29**
Ashbourne Cres.
  TA1: Taun.......................1F **29**
Ash Cl. TA6: B'wtr 1B **14**
Ash Cres. TA1: Taun............2F **27**
Ashford 3A **6**
Ashford Cl. TA6: B'wtr.........3E **13**

Ashford Rd. TA1: Taun 2G **27**
  TA21: Well.....................4D **30**
Ash Gro. Way TA6: B'wtr.......4B **10**
Ashill Cl. TA1: Taun.............3A **28**
Ashleigh Av. TA6: B'wtr........2F **13**
Ashleigh Gdns. TA1: Taun 5A **22**
Ashleigh Ter. TA6: B'wtr.......2F **13**
Ashley Rd. TA1: Taun...........1H **27**
Ashman Way TA6: B'wtr........1D **12**
Ashton Ct. TA1: Taun...........3G **27**
Ashton Rd. TA6: B'wtr..........3F **13**
Aspen Ct. TA6: B'wtr...........1D **12**
Asquith St. TA2: Taun..........3A **22**
Athlone Rd. TA6: B'wtr.........3G **13**
Avalon Rd. TA6: B'wtr..........1B **14**
Avebury Dr. TA6: B'wtr.........6B **10**
Aveline Ct. TA4: Cotf L.........6B **18**
Avenue, The TA1: Taun.........5A **22**
  TA6: B'wtr......................6F **9**
       (off High St.)
Avill Cres. TA1: Taun...........6E **23**
Avon Cl. TA1: Taun..............2H **27**
Axe Rd. TA6: B'wtr..............2H **13**

B

Bacon Dr. TA1: Taun 1E **29**
Badgers Cl. TA1: Bish H 1F **27**
Bagborough Dr. TA6: B'wtr....3F **13**
Bagborough Rd. TA2: Taun 3B **22**
Bagley Green 6A **30**
Bagley Rd. TA21: B Grn 6A **30**
Baileys Ga. TA4: Cotf L.........6A **18**
Bailey St. TA6: B'wtr.................6H **9**
Bakers Cl. TA1: Bish H 1E **27**
Baker's La. TA21: Well.............3E **31**
Baldwin Rd. TA1: Taun 5D **22**
Ball's La. TA5: Wool 1C **16**
Balmoral Ho. TA6: B'wtr 1A **14**
Bannock Drove TA6: P'ton 2A **4**
Banwell Cl. TA1: Taun 6F **23**
Barbers Mead TA2: Taun 3E **23**
Barclay St. TA6: B'wtr..............1G **13**
Barford Cl. TA5: Spax..............6A **6**
Barford Rd. TA5: Spax.............6A **6**
Barhams Cl. TA6: B'wtr............5G **9**
Barle Cl. TA1: Taun 6F **23**
Barlinch Cl. TA2: Taun.............3D **22**
Barn Meads Rd.
 TA21: Well......................5D **30**
Barr 5C **20**
Barrington Cl. TA1: Taun 4F **27**
Barrow Dr. TA1: Taun 5G **23**
Barrows Cl. TA6: B'wtr............3E **13**
Bartlett Cl. TA1: Taun 3F **27**
Barton Cl. TA1: Taun...............1H **27**
Barton Grn. TA3: Trull 5G **27**
Barton Hey TA4: Bish L 3C **18**
Barton La. TA3: Bish L 5B **24**
Bartons, The TA4: Bish L 2B **18**
Batch Cl. TA7: P'ton 3C **4**
Batch Rd. TA7: P'ton 1B **4**
Bath Bri. Bus. Pk.
 TA6: B'wtr 5H **9**
Bath Ho. TA1: Taun 1A **28**
Bath Pl. TA1: Taun 1B **28**
Bathpool 4G **23**
Bathpool La. TA1: Taun 5E **23**
Bath Rd. TA6: B'wtr 6H **9**
Batts Pk. TA1: Taun 3H **27**
Bawden Cl. TA7: Wlvgtn 4G **5**
Bawdrip 1G **11**
Bawdrip La. TA7: B'drip 1G **11**
Bayford Rd. TA6: B'wtr...........5A **10**
Baymead Cl. TA6: N Peth 2E **17**
Baymead La. TA6: N Peth 3E **17**
Baymead Mdw.
 TA6: N Peth....................3E **17**
Baynes Cl. TA21: Well 2E **31**
Beadon Rd. TA1: Taun............5E **23**
Beauford Cvn. Pk.
 TA2: Nort F.....................4D **20**
Beaufort Rd. TA1: Taun 5A **22**
Beckworth Cl. TA6: B'wtr.......2A **14**
Bedford Cl. TA6: B'wtr............2A **14**
Beech Cl. TA1: Taun 1A **28**
Beech Dr. TA6: B'wtr..............6B **10**
Beech Gro. TA21: Well 3C **30**
Beech Hill TA1: Taun 4E **31**
Beech Rd. TA6: B'wtr.............6B **10**
Beechwood TA6: B'wtr............3E **13**
Beggs Cl. TA6: N Peth 3E **17**
Belgrave Pl. TA1: Taun 4B **22**
Bell Cl. TA6: B'wtr....................6F **9**
Belle Vw. Ter. TA1: Taun 2A **28**
Belmont Cl. TA6: B'wtr...........1B **12**
Belmont Dr. TA6: B'wtr...........2A **28**
Belmont Rd. TA1: Taun 1G **27**
 (in two parts)
Belvedere Cl. TA5: Cann 1F **7**
Belvedes Ct. TA21: Well.........3D **30**
Belvedere Rd. TA1: Taun 5A **22**
Belvedere Trad. Est.
 TA1: Taun 5A **22**
Bernard Taylor Homes
 TA1: Taun 6C **22**
 (off Magdalene St.)
Berry Cl. TA6: B'wtr..............3E **13**
Berrydale Av. TA6: B'wtr 5F **9**
Berwick Cl. TA1: Taun 3G **27**
Bethell Mead TA4: Cotf L.....6A **18**

Beverley Cl. TA2: Taun...........4A **22**
Biddiscombe Cl. TA6: B'wtr....4E **13**
Bilberry Gro. TA1: Taun 4D **28**
Billetfield TA1: Taun 1B **28**
Billet St. TA1: Taun 1B **28**
Bincombe Rd. TA6: B'wtr 1A **14**
Binding Cl. TA6: N Peth 2E **17**
Bindon Rd. TA2: Taun 4F **21**
Binford Pl. TA6: B'wtr.............6G **9**
Bircham Cl. TA6: B'wtr............1C **12**
Bircham Rd. TA2: Taun...........2D **22**
Birch Av. TA7: P'ton 4C **4**
Birch Cl. TA5: Cann 2F **7**
 TA6: B'wtr 6B **10**
Birch Gro. TA1: Taun 5A **22**
Birch Rd. TA21: Well 4E **31**
Bisgood Bldgs. TA6: B'wtr 3A **14**
Bishop Fox Dr. TA1: Taun 2C **28**
Bishops Ct. TA21: Well 3D **30**
Bishop's Hull Hill
 TA1: Bish H...................6F **21**
Bishop's Hull Rd.
 TA1: Bish H 1E **27**
Bishops Lydeard 3B **18**
Bishops Lydeard Station 4A **18**
 (West Somerset Railway)
Bitham La. TA7: Wlvgtn..........5F **5**
Bitham Wlk. TA7: Wlvgtn.......5H **5**
Blackberry Ct. TA21: Well......5D **30**
Blackbrook Bus. Pk.
 TA1: Taun 6G **23**
Blackbrook Pk. Av.
 TA1: Taun 1G **29**
Blackbrook Pavilion
 Sports Cen.....................2F **29**
Blackbrook Rd. TA1: Taun 5G **23**
Blackbrook Way TA1: Taun 2F **29**
Blackdown Rd. TA2: Taun......2D **22**
 TA6: B'wtr 1A **14**
 TA3: R Grn 5B **30**
Blackdown Vw.
 TA2: Nort F.....................3D **20**
Black Horse La. TA1: Taun.....5B **22**
Blacklands TA6: B'wtr..............6F **9**
Blackmoor Rd. TA2: Taun 6H **9**
 TA21: Well 4E **31**
Blackmore La. TA5: Cann 3C **6**
Blackthorn Cl. TA6: N Peth.....3E **17**
Blackthorn Gdns.
 TA1: Taun 2C **22**
Blagdon Cres. TA1: Taun 3H **27**
Blake Gdns. TA6: B'wtr...........1C **12**
 (off St Saviour's Av.)
Blake Ind. Pk. TA6: B'wtr.......2G **13**
Blake Pl. TA6: B'wtr.................6G **9**
Blakes La. TA5: Wemb............4C **8**
Blakes Rd. TA6: Wemb...........4D **8**
Blake St. TA1: Taun 6D **22**
 TA1: Taun 1F **13**
Blenheim Rd. TA1: Taun 5F **23**
 TA6: B'wtr 4B **10**
Bloomfield Cl. TA1: Taun 6E **23**
Bloom Row TA6: B'wtr............6B **10**
Blossom Cl. TA6: B'wtr...........6A **10**
Bluebell Cl. TA1: Taun............4E **29**
Bluett Rd. TA21: Well..............5D **30**
Blythe Cl. TA1: Taun 3H **27**
Boards Rd. TA6: B'wtr.............5G **9**
Bodmin Rd. TA2: Taun 2C **22**
Bond St. TA6: B'wtr..................6F **9**
Boons Orchard TA3: Ruish 6A **24**
Booth Way TA6: Wemb............6D **8**
Bossington Dr. TA2: Taun.......2D **22**
Bourne Gro. TA1: Taun 1F **29**
Bouverie Rd. TA6: B'wtr..........6D **8**
Bovet Cl. TA1: Taun 3F **27**
Bovet St. TA21: Well................3C **30**
Bower Av. TA6: B'wtr...............5A **10**
Bowerings Rd. TA6: B'wtr 3E **13**
Bower La. TA6: E Bwr 4B **10**
Bower Mnr. Shop. Cen.
 TA6: B'wtr 5B **10**
Bowfell Cl. TA1: Taun 3G **27**
Bowline Ct. TA6: Wemb 4E **9**
Bowling Grn. TA5: Cann 1F **7**
Bowmont Gro. TA1: Taun 5E **15**
Bowood Rd. TA2: Taun............4C **22**
Bradbeers TA3: Trull................6G **27**
Bradfield Cl. TA6: B'wtr 4E **13**

Bradford Cl. TA1: Taun 4G **27**
Bradley Green 3E **7**
Bradney 3F **11**
Bradney La. TA7: B'drip..........2D **10**
Bramble Pk. TA1: Taun 2E **29**
Brambles, The TA21: Well 5D **30**
Bramley Rd. TA1: Taun 5F **23**
Branksome Av. TA6: B'wtr......6H **9**
Brantwood Rd. TA6: Wemb....5C **8**
Brendon Rd. TA6: B'wtr..........5F **9**
 TA21: Well 2C **30**
Brendons TA4: Bish L.............4B **18**
Brendon Way TA6: B'wtr.........5F **9**
Brentsfield La. TA7: C'zoy......1F **15**
Brewhouse Theatre &
 Arts Cen. 6B **22**
Briant Cl. TA1: Taun 3F **27**
Bridge St. TA1: Taun...............6B **22**
Bridge, The TA1: Taun............6B **22**
Bridgwater 6F **9**
Bridgwater Station 1H **13**
Bridgwater Arts Cen. 6B **22**
 (off Castle St.)
BRIDGWATER COMMUNITY
 HOSPITAL.....................6G **9**
Bridgwater Ent. Cen.
 TA6: B'wtr 6F **9**
Bridgwater Rd. TA1: Taun 6F **23**
 TA2: B'pool 4G **23**
 TA6: N Peth 2E **17**
Brigg Cl. TA6: Wemb..............4E **9**
Brimstone La.
 TA21: Samp A 6A **30**
Brindle Cl. TA2: Taun..............4G **21**
Bristol Rd.
 TA6: B'wtr, D'ball............5A **4**
Brittons Ash TA2: B'pool 2H **23**
Broadguage Bus. Pk.
 TA4: Bish L 4A **18**
Broadlands Av. TA6: N Peth ..2E **17**
Broadlands La. TA5: Durl.......1A **12**
Broadlands Ri. TA1: Taun 2A **28**
Broadlands Rd. TA1: Taun 2A **28**
Broadlands Way TA1: Taun 2A **28**
Broadlawn TA7: Wlvgtn 4H **5**
Broadly Gdns.
 TA2: Monk H 1G **23**
Broadoak Rd. TA6: B'wtr........6B **10**
Broadstone TA7: W'land.........5H **15**
Broadway TA6: B'wtr...............1F **13**
Brook Cl. TA6: N Peth 3D **16**
Brooke Rd. TA1: Taun 6D **22**
Brooklands Rd. TA6: B'wtr......6A **10**
Brooklands Rd.
 TA21: R Grn 4B **30**
Brook La. TA5: Cann 2F **7**
 TA7: B'drip 1H **11**
Brookside Cl. TA3: Trull 5H **27**
Brooks Pl. TA21: Well.............3E **31**
Brook St. TA5: Cann 1F **7**
 TA7: N New 6E **17**
Broomfield Ho. TA2: Taun 3A **22**
Broughton Cl. TA1: Taun 2E **29**
Broughton La.
 TA3: Shore, Stoke M 5E **29**
Broughton Pk. Res. Homes
 TA3: Shore.....................5F **29**
Brownings Rd. TA5: Cann......2F **7**
Brue Av. TA6: B'wtr.................2G **13**
Bruford Cl. TA1: Taun 1A **28**
Brunel Ct. TA6: B'wtr..............5F **9**
 (off Waverley Rd.)
Bryer Cl. TA6: B'wtr................4E **13**
Brymore Rd. TA6: B'wtr..........6D **8**
Buces Rd. TA1: Taun 3F **27**
Buckingham Cl. TA6: B'wtr.....3G **13**
Buckland Rd. TA2: Taun 3D **22**
Buckwell TA21: Well................3E **31**
Bulford Cl. TA6: B'wtr.............4D **30**
Bulford La. TA21: Well............4D **30**
Bull Horn Drove
 TA7: W'land 5E **15**
Bull Mdw. TA4: Bish L............4C **18**
Bull St. TA3: Creech M...........5C **24**
Bune Vs. TA6: Wemb..............4E **9**
Bungalows, The
 TA2: Monk H 1H **23**
Burchills Cl. TA21: West 3A **30**
Burchill's Hill
 TA21: Tone, West............3A **30**

C

Burch's Cl. TA1: Taun 2G **27**
Burgage TA21: Well.................3D **30**
Burge Cres. TA4: Cotf L.........6A **18**
Burge Mdw. TA4: Cotf L 6A **18**
Burgess Cl. TA1: Taun 3F **27**
Burnshill Dr. TA2: Nort F 3E **21**
Burns Rd. TA1: Taun 6E **23**
Burrough Way TA21: Well 5C **30**
Burton Pl. TA1: Taun 1A **28**
Bushy Cross La.
 TA3: Ruish......................6A **24**
Bussex..................................1G **15**
Bussex Sq. TA7: W'land.........1G **15**
Butleigh Cl. TA6: B'wtr...........1B **14**
Butts Corner TA6: N Peth.......2E **17**
Byron Rd. TA1: Taun 1E **29**

C

Cadeside Cvn. Site
 TA21: Poole 2F **31**
Calder Cres. TA1: Taun...........6F **23**
Calvados Rd. TA1: Taun 1C **28**
Calway Rd. TA1: Taun 3C **28**
Cambridge Ter. TA2: Taun......2C **22**
Camden Rd. TA6: B'wtr...........6E **9**
Campion Dr. TA1: Taun 3E **29**
Canal Cl. TA21: Tone..............1A **28**
Canal Rd. TA1: Taun 5B **22**
Canal Ter. TA1: Taun 5B **22**
Cannington 1F **7**
Cannington Countryside
 Vis. Cen. 1F **7**
Canns La. TA6: N Peth 2E **17**
 TA7: P'ton 3C **4**
Cann St. TA1: Taun 1A **28**
Canon St. TA1: Taun 6B **22**
Canworth Way TA6: B'wtr 2A **14**
Capes Cl. TA6: B'wtr...............6G **9**
Caradon Pl. TA6: B'wtr 4F **9**
Caray Gro. TA3: Creech M.....4C **24**
Carlton Dr. TA6: B'wtr 4F **9**
Carpenters Cl. TA3: Ruish 6B **24**
Carvers Rd. TA6: B'wtr............6G **9**
Cashford Ga. TA2: Taun..........3E **23**
Castle Bow TA1: Taun 6B **22**
Castle Cotts. TA1: C'ston 2H **31**
Castle Fld. Ind. Est.
 TA6: B'wtr 5G **9**
Castlefield La.
 TA4: Comey....................5C **26**
Castle Grn. TA1: Taun 6B **22**
Castlemans Rd. TA1: Taun......3F **27**
Castle Moat TA6: B'wtr...........6F **9**
Castle Rd. TA21: C'ston 2H **31**
Castle Sports Cen., The 6H **21**
Castle St. TA1: Taun 6A **22**
 TA6: B'wtr 6F **9**
Castle Wlk. TA1: Taun 6B **22**
Castle Way TA1: Taun 6B **22**
Cats La. TA2: Ched F..............1C **22**
Causeway TA7: Wlvgtn 1H **5**
Causeway Cl. TA7: Wlvgtn......3H **5**
Cecil Ter. TA1: Taun 1H **13**
Cedar Cl. TA1: Taun 1F **29**
 TA6: B'wtr 2A **14**
Cedar Ct. TA21: Well 4E **31**
Celandine Mead TA1: Taun 4E **29**
Cellophane Bus. Pk.
 TA6: B'wtr 4A **10**
Chad's Hill TA5: Cann.............1E **7**
Chaffinch Cl. TA1: Bish H.......6F **9**
Chalice M. TA6: B'wtr..............6F **9**
Chamberlain Ho.
 TA1: Taun 5H **21**
Chamberlain Av. TA6: B'wtr....5A **10**
Champford La. TA21: Well......4D **30**
Champford M. TA21: Well........4D **30**
Chandos St. TA6: B'wtr...........6F **9**
Chantry Cl. TA2: Taun 3D **22**
Chapel St. TA4: Bish L 2B **18**
Chapel La. TA6: B'wtr..............1G **13**
Chapman Ct. TA1: Taun..........3G **27**
Charles Cres. TA1: Taun 5F **23**
Charlton 2F **25**
Charlton Cl. TA6: B'wtr 1A **14**
Charlton La. TA3: Creech M....3E **25**
Charlton Rd.
 TA3: Creech H, Durs 1D **24**

Charlynch 5B 6
Charlynch Hill TA5: Charl........5B 6
Charlynch La.
　TA5: Cann, Charl........5F 7
Charlynch Rd.
　TA5: Charl, Spax........6A 6
Charnwood Cl. TA6: B'wter.....4F 9
Charter Wlk. TA1: Taun.....5E 23
Chatham Av. TA6: B'wtr.....5E 9
Chaucer Cl. TA6: N Peth.....2E 17
Cheats Rd. TA3: Ruish.....5A 24
Cheddon Fitzpaine 1E 23
Cheddon M. TA2: Taun.....3B 22
Cheddon Rd. TA2: Taun.....4B 22
Chedzoy 5F 11
Chedzoy La.
　TA7: C'zoy, E Bwr........3C 10
Cheer La. TA7: W'land.....1G 15
Chelmer Cl. TA1: Taun.....6F 23
Chelston 2G 31
Chelston Heathfield 2H 31
Chelston Ter. TA21: C'ston...2H 31
Chelwood Dr. TA1: Taun.....3A 28
Chepstow Av. TA6: B'wtr.....3G 13
Cherry Cl. TA6: B'wtr.....2A 14
Cherry Gro. TA2: Taun.....4B 22
Cherry Orchard TA1: Trull...5H 27
Cherry Tree La. TA1: Taun...3B 28
Chertsey Cl. TA7: Wlvgtn....3G 5
Chestnut Cl. TA6: B'wtr.....1A 14
　TA21: Well.....4E 31
Chestnut Dr. TA1: Taun.....4E 29
Cheyne Wlk. TA1: Taun.....1B 28
Chidgey Cl. TA6: B'wtr.....6F 9
Chilliswood Cres.
　TA1: Taun.....2F 27
Chilliswood La. TA3: Trull...6C 26
Chilpitts TA7: Wlvgtn.....3H 5
Chilton Cl. TA6: B'wtr.....4F 9
Chilton Moor La.
　TA6: Chil T.....4F 9
Chilton Pk. Res. Cvn. Pk.
　TA6: Chil T.....4F 9
Chilton Rd. TA5: Chil T.....3F 9
　TA6: B'wtr, Chil T.....4F 9
Chilton St. TA6: B'wtr.....4F 9
Chilton Trinity 2F 9
Chip La. TA1: Taun.....4A 22
　(in two parts)
Church Cl. TA2: Nort F.....4D 20
Church Fld. La. TA7: P'ton....3B 4
　(in two parts)
Church Flds. TA21: Well 2D 30
　(in two parts)
Churchill Way TA1: Taun.....2A 28
Church La. TA3: Ruish.....5A 24
　TA7: W'land.....2G 15
Church Mdw. TA6: B'wtr.....5E 9
Church Pas. TA6: B'wtr.....1F 13
　(off St Mary St.)
Church Path TA6: B'wtr.....6D 8
Church Rd. TA3: Trull.....5G 27
　TA6: Wemb.....5D 8
　TA7: B'drip.....1G 11
　TA7: N New.....6F 17
Church Sq. TA1: Taun.....6B 22
Church St. TA1: Taun.....1D 28
　TA4: Bish L.....2B 18
　TA5: Cann.....1F 7
　TA6: B'wtr.....6G 9
　TA7: Wlvgtn.....3H 5
Church Vw. TA5: Chil T.....2F 9
Church Wlk. TA6: N Peth.....3D 16
Claremont Ct. TA1: Taun.....3G 27
Claremont Dr. TA1: Taun.....2F 27
Claremont Gro. TA6: B'wtr...5B 10
Claremont La. TA1: Taun.....3G 27
Clarence Dr. TA6: N Peth.....2E 17
Clarence St. TA1: Taun.....6A 22
Clare St. TA6: B'wtr.....6F 9
　(in two parts)
　TA6: N Peth.....2E 17
Clark Cl. TA7: Wlvgtn.....4H 5
Clarks Rd. TA1: Taun.....1H 13
Cleeve Rd. TA2: Taun.....3D 22
Cleveland St. TA1: Taun.....6A 22
Clifford Ashman Ct.
　TA2: Taun.....4A 22
Clifford Av. TA2: Taun.....2A 22
Clifford Cres. TA2: Taun.....2A 22

Clifford Lodge TA5: Cann.....1F 7
Clifford M. TA21: Well.....3E 31
Clifford Pk. TA5: Cann.....1E 7
Clifford Ter. TA21: Well.....3D 30
Cliff Rd. TA6: N Peth.....4B 16
Clifton Ter. TA1: Taun.....4B 22
Clink, The TA6: B'wtr.....6F 9
Clipper Cl. TA6: B'wtr.....1A 14
Clover Mead TA1: Taun.....4E 29
Cloverton Dr. TA6: B'wtr.....4B 10
Coal Orchard TA1: Taun.....6B 22
Cob Castle TA21: Ham.....2H 31
Cole Cl. TA4: Cotf L.....5A 18
Coleridge Cres. TA1: Taun.....1D 28
　(off Coleridge Rd.)
Coleridge Grn. TA1: Taun.....1D 28
Coleridge Rd. TA6: B'wtr.....5E 9
Coleridge Sq. TA6: B'wtr.....5E 9
Colin Av. TA2: Taun.....2B 22
Colin Rd. TA2: Taun.....3B 22
College Rd. TA2: Taun.....4H 21
College Vw. TA1: Taun.....2G 27
College Way TA1: Taun.....4G 27
　TA6: B'wtr.....5H 9
Colley La. TA1: Taun.....1H 13
Colley La. Ind. Est.
　TA6: B'wtr.....2H 13
Collingwood Ct. TA6: B'wtr 6F 9
　(off Drakes Cl.)
Colman Rd. TA1: Taun.....3F 27
Colmer Rd. TA6: B'wtr.....4F 9
Combe La. TA7: Wlvgtn.....4H 5
Comeytrowe 3F 27
Comeytrowe Cen.
　TA1: Taun.....3G 27
Comeytrowe Ind. Est.
　TA4: Comey.....3E 27
Comeytrowe La. TA1: Taun ...3F 27
　(nr. Queensway)
　TA1: Taun.....2E 27
　(nr. Stonegallows)
Comeytrowe Orchard
　TA1: Taun.....2E 27
Comeytrowe Ri. TA1: Taun....2F 27
Comeytrowe Rd. TA1: Taun....3F 27
　TA3: Trull.....3F 27
　TA4: Taun, Trull.....3F 27
Compass 6F 13
Compass Hill TA1: Taun.....1A 28
Compass Ri. TA1: Taun.....1A 28
Compton Cl. TA2: Taun.....4C 22
Condell Cl. TA6: B'wtr.....4F 9
Connaught Ho. TA6: B'wtr.....6A 10
Conway Rd. TA5: Cann.....1F 7
Cooks Cl. TA3: Creech M.....3C 24
Cook Way TA2: Taun.....4G 21
Coopers Mill TA2: Nort F.....4D 20
Coplestons St. TA3: Trull.....4H 27
Copper Beeches TA1: Taun ...2E 27
Coppin Rd. TA2: Nort F.....4D 20
Copse, The TA6: B'wtr.....6B 10
Corams La. TA21: Well 3B 30
Corkscrew La.
　TA2: Staple, Taun.....2H 21
Cormorant Cl. TA6: B'wtr.....2A 14
Cornborough Pl. TA6: B'wtr....6H 9
Corner Cl. TA21: Well.....5D 30
Cornhill TA6: B'wtr.....1F 13
　TA21: Well.....3D 30
Cornishway E. TA1: Taun.....1F 27
Cornishway Nth. TA1: Taun....1F 27
Cornishway Sth. TA1: Taun....2F 27
Cornishway W. TA1: Taun.....1F 27
Coronation Cl. TA3: Ruish.....6B 24
Coronation Ho. TA6: B'wtr.....5A 10
Coronation Rd. TA1: Taun.....6E 9
Corporation St. TA1: Taun.....1B 28
Cory Rd. TA7: P'ton.....2C 22
Cossington La.
　TA7: Coss, Wlvgtn.....5H 5
Cotford St Luke 6A 18
Cothelstone Cl. TA6: B'wtr....1B 12
Cothelstone Rd.
　TA4: Bish L.....1B 18
Cotlake Cl. TA1: Taun.....3B 28
Cotlake Ri. TA1: Taun.....4A 28
Countess Av. TA6: B'wtr.....5H 9
County Wlk. TA1: Taun.....1B 28
Court Dr. TA21: Well.....3C 30
Court Gro. TA7: P'ton.....3C 4

Court Hill TA1: Taun.....2H 27
Courtland Rd. TA21: Well 3D 30
Court Orchard TA5: Cann.....2F 7
Court Rd. TA2: Nort F.....4C 20
Court St. TA6: B'wtr.....6F 9
Courtway Av. TA6: B'wtr.....1A 14
Cowleaze Drove TA3: Ruish...6C 24
Cox Rd. TA21: Well.....5C 30
Crabtrees Cvn. Pk.
　TA5: Cann.....1F 7
Craig Lea TA2: Taun.....3A 22
Cranbourne Cl. TA6: B'wtr.....5F 9
Crancombe La.
　TA7: Kwle, Wlvgtn.....6F 5
Cranes Cl. TA2: Taun.....3F 23
Cranleigh Gdns.
　TA6: B'wtr.....1G 13
Cranmer Rd. TA1: Taun.....6C 22
Cranwell Cl. TA5: Wool.....1D 16
Crawlic La. TA4: Bish L.....1B 18
Creechbarrow Rd.
　TA1: Taun.....5E 23
Creechberry Orchard
　TA1: Taun.....5F 23
Creech Bus. Pk.
　TA3: Creech M.....5B 24
Creech Heathfield 1D 24
Creech Mill Ind. Units
　TA3: Creech M.....5B 24
Creech St Michael 4C 24
Creechwood Ter. TA3: Creech M
　.....3D 24
Crescent, The TA1: Taun.....1A 28
Crescent Way TA1: Taun.....1B 28
Cresswell Av. TA2: Taun.....3H 21
Crestfield Av. TA6: B'wtr.....4F 9
Cridlands Mdw. TA6: Wemb...5E 9
Crockers Hill TA7: Wlvgtn.....3G 5
Cromwell Rd. TA1: Taun.....5D 22
　TA6: B'wtr.....3G 13
Crossacre TA6: Wemb.....5D 8
Crossfield Cl. TA6: Wemb.....5D 8
Cross Keys TA2: Nort F.....2E 21
Cross Keys Cl. TA2: Nort F....3E 21
Crosslands TA21: Tone.....1B 30
Crossmead TA7: Wlvgtn.....4H 5
Cross Vw. Ri. TA6: Wemb.....5D 8
Crossway TA1: Taun.....5E 23
Crossways Rd. TA6: B'wtr.....4H 13
Crosswell Cl. TA6: N Peth.....3D 16
Crowcombe Rd. TA1: Taun.....3B 22
Crowcombe Wlk.
　TA6: B'wtr.....1C 12
Crown Cl. TA2: Taun.....4E 23
Crown Ind. Est. TA2: Taun.....4E 23
Crown La. TA3: Creech H.....1D 24
Crown Wlk. TA1: Taun.....1B 28
Crowpill La. TA6: B'wtr.....5F 9
Crow's La. TA6: E Bwr.....4C 10
　(in two parts)
　TA7: E Bwr.....5C 10
Crufts Mdw.
　TA3: Creech M.....4B 24
Crypton Technology Bus. Pk.
　TA6: B'wtr.....3H 9
Culmhead Cl. TA1: Taun.....3H 27
Culverhay Cl. TA7: P'ton.....3C 4
Currymoor Drove
　TA1: N Curry.....3H 25
Currypool La. TA5: Cann.....4A 6
Curvalion Gdns.
　TA3: Creech M.....4C 24
Curvalion Rd.
　TA3: Creech M.....4C 24
Cushuish 1H 19
Cutliff Cl. TA1: Taun.....3A 28
Cypress Dr. TA7: P'ton.....4C 4
Cyril St. TA2: Taun.....4A 22
Cyril St. W. TA2: Taun.....4A 22

Dabinett Cl. TA2: Nort F.....3D 20
Dampiet St. TA6: B'wtr.....1F 13
Dancing Hill TA6: N Peth 2B 16
Danesboro Rd. TA6: B'wtr.....1C 12
Darby Way TA4: Bish L.....1C 18
Dare Cl. TA2: Taun.....2C 22

Darkfield Way TA7: Wlvgtn....5G 5
Dark La. TA21: Well.....4D 30
Darwin Cl. TA2: Taun.....3F 21
Davis Cl. TA6: B'wtr.....3F 13
Dawbins Dr. TA7: Wlvgtn.....3H 5
Daws Cl. TA6: B'wtr.....4E 13
Daws La. TA6: N Peth.....4D 16
Daws Mead TA1: Bish H.....1E 27
Deacon Rd. TA6: B'wtr.....5A 10
Deal Cl. TA6: B'wtr.....6B 10
Deane Dr. TA1: Taun.....2F 27
Deane Ga. Av. TA1: Taun.....5G 23
Deane Ga. Office Pk.
　TA1: Taun.....6G 23
Dellers Ct. TA1: Taun.....5B 22
Deller's Wharf TA1: Taun.....5B 22
Delta Ri. TA4: Bish L.....1B 18
Dene Rd.
　TA4: Bish L, Cotf L.....6A 18
Denman's La. TA5: Cann.....2F 7
Denmark Ter. TA2: Taun.....3B 22
Denning Cl. TA1: Taun.....3F 27
Derwent Gro. TA1: Taun.....6F 23
Devonia Pk. Homes
　TA4: R'well.....3A 26
Devonshire St. TA6: B'wtr.....6H 9
Dillons Rd. TA3: Creech M.....4C 24
Dinhams TA3: Ruish.....5B 24
Dipford 6E 27
Dipford Rd. TA3: Trull.....6E 27
Disraeli Pl. TA1: Taun.....5H 21
Dobree Pk. TA21: R Grn.....4A 30
Dorchester Rd. TA2: Taun.....2C 22
Dorset Rd. TA6: B'wtr.....2A 14
Dosters La. TA2: W Monk.....1A 24
Dovai Dr. TA6: Wemb.....4E 9
Dover Rd. TA2: Taun.....2C 22
Dovetail Ct. TA1: Taun.....1A 28
Dowell Cl. TA2: Taun.....4G 21
Down End 4A 4
Downend Cres. TA6: P'ton.....4A 4
Downend Rd. TA6: P'ton.....4A 4
Downend Ter. TA6: P'ton.....4A 4
Downhall Dr. TA6: Wemb.....5D 8
Dowslands 3D 28
Dowsland Way TA1: Taun.....3E 29
Drake Cl. TA2: Taun.....3F 21
Drakes Cl. TA3: Ruish.....5A 24
　TA6: B'wtr.....6F 9
Drakes Pk. TA21: Well.....2D 30
Drakes Pk. Nth.
　TA21: Well.....2D 30
Drawbridge Ho. TA6: B'wtr....5F 9
Draycott Av. TA6: B'wtr.....4C 22
Drive, The TA1: Taun.....3H 27
　TA7: Wlvgtn.....3H 5
Drove, The TA6: B'wtr.....5G 9
Duchess Cl. TA6: B'wtr.....4E 9
Duke Av. TA5: Cann.....2F 7
Dukes Mead TA6: B'wtr.....3G 13
Duke St. TA1: Taun.....1C 28
　TA6: B'wtr.....5E 9
Dunball 5A 4
Dunball Drove TA6: D'ball.....4A 4
Dunball Ind. Est. TA6: D'ball....4A 4
Duncombe Cl. TA6: B'wtr.....6B 10
Dunkerton Ri. TA2: Nort F.....3D 20
Dunkery Rd. TA6: B'wtr.....1C 12
Dunkleys Way TA1: Taun.....2E 29
Dunster Cl. TA2: Taun.....3D 22
Dunwear 3B 14
Dunwear Ho. TA6: B'wtr.....1A 14
Dunwear La. TA6: D'wear.....3B 14
Durham Pl. TA2: Taun.....2C 22
Durleigh 2B 12
Durleigh Cl. TA6: B'wtr.....1D 12
Durleigh Hill TA5: Durl.....3A 12
Durleigh Rd. TA6: B'wtr.....1B 12
Durston Way TA1: Taun.....3A 28
Dyers Grn. TA6: N Peth.....3E 17
Dyer's La.
　TA2: B'pool, Monk H.....3G 23

Earl's Cl. TA6: B'wtr.....4E 9
E. Approach Rd. TA7: P'ton....3F 5
Eastbourne Ct. TA1: Taun.....6C 22
　(off Eastbourne Rd.)

Eastbourne Ga. TA1: Taun......6C 22
Eastbourne Rd. TA1: Taun......6C 22
Eastbourne Ter. TA1: Taun 6C 22
East Bower 5B 10
Eastbrook Ter. TA3: Trull......5H 27
Eastern Av. TA6: B'wtr..........1B 14
Eastgate Gdns. TA1: Taun 6C 22
Eastleigh Rd. TA1: Taun 1D 28
East Lydeard 2D 18
Eastover 6G 9
Eastover TA6: B'wtr..............6G 9
East Quay TA6: B'wtr............6G 9
E. Quay M. TA6: B'wtr...........5F 9
East Reach TA1: Taun 6C 22
Eastside La. TA7: B'drip 2G 11
East St. TA1: Taun 1B 28
  TA5: Cann................1F 7
Eastwick Av. TA2: Taun 3B 22
Eastwick Rd. TA2: Taun 3C 22
Eastwood Cl. TA6: B'wtr 1A 14
Eaton Cres. TA2: Taun 4C 22
Edgebury TA7: Wlvgtn..........4H 5
Edinburgh Rd. TA6: B'wtr......3E 13
Edward St. TA6: B'wtr...........6G 9
Eight Acre La. TA21: Well......4D 30
Eight Acre Mdw.
  TA6: Wemb................5E 9
Eldergrove Cl. TA6: B'wtr......4B 10
  (off Ash Gro. Way)
Eleven Ct. TA6: B'wtr...........1E 13
Elizabeth Ho. TA1: Taun.......2B 28
  (off Wilton Orchard)
Elizabeth Way TA6: B'wtr......1A 14
Ellen Cl. TA6: N Peth...........2C 30
Ellis Gro. TA2: Nort F 3C 20
Elm Gro. TA1: Taun 5A 22
Elmgrove Cl. TA6: B'wtr 4B 10
Elm La. TA7: Wlvgtn 4H 5
Elm Lea Cl. TA7: P'ton 4C 4
Elm Pk. TA1: Taun 5A 22
Elms Cl. TA1: Taun 5A 22
Elms Est. TA2: Monk H 2H 23
Elmside Ho. TA6: B'wtr 3F 13
Elmside Rd. TA6: B'wtr 2E 13
Elms Pde. TA1: Taun 5A 22
Elms Rd. TA21: Well 4F 21
Elm Ter. TA2: Taun 4H 21
Elmwood Av. TA6: B'wtr 2F 13
Elworthy Dr. TA21: Well 5D 30
Enmore Rd. TA2: Taun 3B 22
  TA5: Durl................2A 12
Escott Ct. TA6: B'wtr...........5F 9
Essex Dr. TA1: Taun 3G 27
Ethpark Gro. TA2: Taun 4B 22
Evesham Dr. TA6: B'wtr 4G 13
Feversham Way
  TA2: Taun................2D 22
Exeter Rd. TA21:
  B Grn, R Grn, Well 6A 30
Exeter Rd. Cvn. Pk.
  TA21: R Grn 5A 30
Express Pk. TA6: B'wtr........2H 9

F

Fairfax Cl. TA6: B'wtr..........5A 10
Fairfax Rd. TA6: B'wtr..........5A 10
Fairfield Rd. TA2: Taun 2D 22
Fairwater Cl. TA2: Taun 4H 21
Fairways Camping Site, The
  TA7: B'drip 6H 5
Fairways, The TA1: Taun 3B 28
Falcon Cl. TA1: Bish H 6G 21
Farm Vw. TA1: Taun 1C 22
Farrant Cl. TA1: Bish H 6E 21
Farriers Grn. TA2: Monk H 3H 23
Farthing Rd. TA6: B'wtr........4E 13
Farthings Pitts TA21: Well.....5C 30
Fennington 2G 19
Fennington La.
  TA2: King L...............3G 19
Ferndale Dr. TA1: Taun 4H 27
Ferndown Cl. TA1: Taun 3H 27
Fernleigh Av. TA6: B'wtr......2F 13
Feversham Av. TA6: B'wtr.....5E 9
Feversham Way
  TA2: Taun................2D 22
Field La. TA7: B'drip...........6G 5
Fields End TA1: Taun 2E 29
Firepool 5C 22
Firtree Cl. TA6: B'wtr 1B 14

Fitzroy 6G 19
Fivash Cl. TA1: Taun 4G 27
Five Yards TA4: Bish L 3C 18
Fletcher Cl. TA2: Taun 2D 22
Florence Cl. TA6: Wemb 4E 9
Florence Rd. TA2: Taun 4B 22
Folly Cl. TA5: Cann 1F 7
Fons George TA1: Taun 2A 28
  (in two parts)
Fons George Cl.
  TA1: Taun................2A 28
Fons George Rd.
  TA1: Taun................2A 28
Footlands Cl. TA1: Taun 3B 28
Ford St. TA21: Well............5F 31
Fore St. TA1: Taun 1B 28
  TA5: Cann................1F 7
  TA6: B'wtr................6F 9
  TA6: N Peth..............3D 16
  TA7: W'land..............5H 15
  TA21: Well...............4D 30
Foundry Rd. TA1: Taun 6B 22
Four Acre Mead
  TA4: Bish L...............3C 18
Four Acre Mdw. TA6: B'wtr.....5E 9
Fouracres Cl. TA1: Taun 3D 28
Four Forks 6A 6
Four Forks La. TA5: Spax......6A 6
Fowler's Mead Drove
  TA7: D'wear..............4D 14
Fowler's Plot 1F 15
Fowler St. TA2: Taun 4A 22
Fox Brothers Ind. Est.
  TA2: Tone................2C 30
Fox Cl. TA21: West...........3A 30
Foxdown Hill TA21: Well......5C 30
Foxdown Ter. TA21: Well 5D 30
Foxhole La.
  TA3: Creech M............4D 24
Frampton Rd. TA6: B'wtr......3F 13
Francis Bastin Ho.
  TA6: N Peth..............3D 16
  (off Fore St.)
Francis Cl. TA3: Creech H......2D 24
Francis Reed Cl.
  TA7: W'land..............2G 15
Francolin Cl. TA1: Taun 4A 28
Franklin Cl. TA2: Taun 4F 21
Franks Cl. TA1: Taun 5H 21
Frank Webber Rd.
  TA21: R Grn 4A 30
Frederick Rd. TA6: B'wtr......5A 10
Fremantle Rd. TA2: Taun 3D 28
French Weir Av.
  TA1: Taun................5A 22
French Weir Cl. TA1: Taun.....6A 22
Frethey Rd. TA4: Bish H 6D 20
Friarn Av. TA6: B'wtr..........1F 13
Friarn Lawn TA6: B'wtr.........1F 13
Friarn St. TA6: B'wtr...........1F 13
Frieze Hill 5H 21
Frobisher Way TA2: Taun 4F 21
Front St. TA7: C'zoy...........6E 11
Fry's La. TA7: C'zoy...........6G 11
Fullands Av. TA1: Taun 4D 28
Fullands Ct. TA1: Taun 3D 28
Fullands Rd. TA1: Taun 3D 28
Fulwood Cl. TA1: Taun 3H 27
Furlong Grn. TA3: Trull 4G 27
Furlongs Av. TA6: B'wtr.......3E 13
Furze Cl. TA6: B'wtr 1D 12

G

Gables, The TA21: Well........3C 30
Galmington 2G 27
Galmington Cl. TA1: Taun 1G 27
Galmington Dr. TA1: Taun 2F 27
Galmington La. TA1: Taun 2G 27
Galmington Rd. TA1: Taun 1G 27
Galmington Trad. Est.
  TA1: Taun................1F 27
Garden Ter. TA1: Tone.........1B 28
Garden Wlk. TA6: B'wtr........3E 13
Gatchell Grn. TA3: Trull 5G 27
Gatchell Mdw. TA3: Trull 5G 27
Gaunton Cl. TA2: Taun 2H 27
Gay Cl. TA21: Well............3E 31
Gay St. TA21: Well............3E 31

Gelosia Cl. TA7: W'land.......1G 15
George St. TA2: Taun 4B 22
  (in two parts)
  TA6: B'wtr................6F 9
  TA21: Well...............3D 30
George Williams Ct.
  TA6: B'wtr................1F 13
Gerbestone La.
  TA21: C'ston, Well.........6G 31
Gibb Ho. TA6: B'wtr...........3E 13
Gillards TA1: Bish H 6F 21
Gillards Cl. TA21: R Grn 5B 30
Gill Cres. TA1: Taun...........3F 27
Gipsy La. TA1: Bish H.........1G 27
Gladstone St. TA2: Taun 4A 22
Gladstone Ter. TA1: Taun 3E 31
Glanfield Cl. TA4: Bish L 2B 18
Glasses Mead TA1: Taun 3F 27
Glen Cl. TA2: Nort F 2D 20
Glen Dr. TA2: Taun 2C 22
Glenthorne Rd. TA2: Taun 4B 22
Glenwood Gdns.
  TA2: Taun................2B 22
Gloucester Rd. TA6: B'wtr......3F 13
Gloucester St. TA1: Taun 6C 22
Gooch Cl. TA6: B'wtr..........1H 13
Gordon Rd. TA1: Taun.........1C 28
Gordon's Cl. TA1: Taun 3D 28
Gordon Ter. TA6: B'wtr........1G 13
Gore Sq. TA4: Bish L 3B 18
Gort Rd. TA2: Nort F 2C 20
Gothelney Green 6F 7
Grafton Cl. TA1: Taun 2C 28
Graham Way TA4: Cotf L......6A 18
Granary Way TA3: Trull 6H 27
Grange Cl. TA5: Cann 2G 7
  TA21: Well...............4E 31
Grange Dr. TA2: Taun 4C 22
  TA6: B'wtr................2D 12
Grange Gdns. TA2: Taun 3C 22
Grange Rd. TA2: Taun 4C 22
Grange Walk TA2: Taun 4C 22
Grasmere TA6: Wemb 5C 8
Graves Cl. TA7: W'land........1H 13
Grays Av. TA7: W'land.........4H 15
Grays Rd. TA2: Taun 6D 22
Great Mead TA1: Bish H 1F 27
Greatwood Cl. TA6: B'wtr 4G 13
Grebe Cl. TA6: B'wtr..........1H 13
Grebe Dr. TA6: B'wtr..........1H 13
Grebe Rd. TA2: Taun 4D 22
  TA6: B'wtr................1H 13
Greenacre TA6: Wemb 5D 8
Greenbrook Ter. TA1: Taun 6A 22
Grn. Dragon Ct. TA6: B'wtr....1F 13
  (off Penel Orlieu)
Grn. Dragon La. TA6: B'wtr....1F 13
Greenfield La. TA7: B'drip.....1F 11
Greenlands TA1: Taun 2D 28
Green La. TA3: B'pool 3A 24
Green, The TA6: B'wtr.........3E 13
Greenway TA2: Monk H 2G 23
  TA4: Bish L...............3A 18
Greenway Av. TA2: Taun 4A 22
Greenway Cres. TA2: Taun 3A 22
Greenway Rd. TA2: Taun 3H 21
  TA4: Bish L...............4A 18
  TA21: R Grn 4A 30
Grenville Ct. TA1: Taun 5F 9
  (off Waverley Wharf)
Grenville Ho. TA6: B'wtr.......3F 13
  (off Rhode La.)
Grenville Vw. TA4: Cotf L......6A 18
Groats TA4: Bish L 3C 18
Grooms Orchard
  TA21: Well...............4C 30
Grove Dr. TA2: Taun 2B 22
Grove Ter. TA2: Taun 4B 22
Guildford Pl. TA1: Taun 1B 28
Gumbrells Ct. TA6: B'wtr......1G 13
Gurney St. TA5: Cann.........1G 7
Gwynne La. TA1: Taun 1C 28
Gyffarde St. TA1: Taun 6C 22

H

Haddon La. TA6: N Peth......5A 16
Hadworthy La. TA6: N Peth ...6F 13

Hagget Cl. TA6: B'wtr..........4F 13
Haig La. TA2: Nort F 1C 20
Haines Hill 2A 28
Haines Hill TA1: Taun 2A 28
Haines Pk. TA1: Taun 3H 27
Halcon 5F 23
Halesleigh Rd. TA6: B'wtr......6D 8
Hale Way TA1: Taun 3F 23
Hall Rd. TA7: P'ton 4B 4
Halsway TA6: B'wtr............6A 10
Halswell Cl. TA6: B'wtr........1E 13
Halyard Dr. TA6: Wemb........4E 9
Ham 5F 25
  (nr. Creech St Michael)
Ham 1H 31
  (nr. Wellington)
Hamber Lea TA4: Bish L 3C 18
Hamilton Cl. TA1: Taun 6E 23
Hamilton Rd. TA1: Taun 6D 22
Hamlands La. TA21: Ham......1H 31
Ham La. TA7: Wlvgtn..........3G 5
Hamlyn Cl. TA1: Taun 3G 27
Hammet St. TA1: Taun 6B 22
  TA6: N Peth..............3D 16
Hammet's Wlk. TA1: Taun 2A 28
Hammets Wharf TA1: Taun 6B 22
Hamp 2F 13
Hamp Av. TA6: B'wtr..........2F 13
Hamp Brook Way
  TA6: B'wtr................3E 13
Hamp Grn. Ri. TA6: B'wtr......2F 13
Hamp Ind. Est. TA6: B'wtr.....2G 13
Hamp St. TA6: B'wtr..........2F 13
Hampton Cl. TA6: B'wtr.......4B 10
Hamp Ward TA6: B'wtr........2F 13
Ham Rd. TA3: Creech M......5C 24
  TA21: C'ston.............2G 31
Hamrod La. TA7: W'land......5H 15
Hamwood TA1: Bish H 6F 21
Hamwood La. TA3: Trull 6D 26
Hankridge Way TA1: Taun 5G 23
Harcourt St. TA2: Taun 4A 22
Hardings Cl. TA6: N Peth 3E 17
Harnell Cl. TA1: Taun 1E 29
Harp Chase TA1: Taun 3D 28
Hartley Way TA1: Taun 2F 29
Hartrow Cl. TA1: Taun 3A 28
Haseley Cl. TA1: Taun 2H 27
  (off Ferndown Cl.)
Hatchers Ct. TA2: Taun 3B 22
Hawkers Cl. TA5: Cann 2F 7
Hawker's La. TA5: Cann 3F 7
Hawkridge Rd. TA6: B'wtr.....1F 13
Hawthorn Cl. TA6: B'wtr.......1B 14
Hawthorne Rd. TA21: Well 4E 31
Hawthorn Rd. TA1: Taun 5A 10
Haydon 2F 29
Haydon Cl. TA1: Bish H 6F 21
Haydon La. TA1: Taun 2F 29
  TA3: H'don, H'lade, Taun
  ....3D 28
Haydon Rd. TA1: Taun 6C 22
Haygrove La. TA6: B'wtr.......2C 12
Haygrove Pk. Cvn. Pk.
  TA3: Trull................5H 27
Haygrove Rd. TA6: B'wtr......2C 12
Hayne La. TA5: Charl, Spax...6A 6
Haywood Rd. TA1: Taun 2E 29
Hazel Cl. TA1: Taun 3E 29
Hazelwood Dr. TA6: B'wtr 5C 10
Healys Mdw. TA4: Cotf L 5A 18
Heathcombe Rd.
  TA6: B'wtr................1B 12
Heather Cl. TA1: Taun 4E 29
  TA6: B'wtr................2H 13
Heathfield Cl.
  TA3: Creech H............1D 24
  TA6: N Peth..............2E 17
Heathfield Dr.
  TA2: Monk H.............2H 23
Heavitree Way TA2: Taun......4C 22
Hectors Stones TA7: Wlvgtn...3H 5
Hele 1B 26
Henderson Cl. TA1: Taun 2G 27
  (in two parts)
Henley Gro. TA1: Taun 1H 27
Henley Rd. TA1: Taun 1H 27
Herbert St. TA2: Taun 4A 22
Hereford Dr. TA1: Taun 2C 22
Heron Dr. TA1: Bish H 6F 21

Heron Ga.—Magdalene La.

Heron Ga. TA1: Taun............4G **23**
Heron Ga. Office Pk.
TA1: Taun........................5G **23**
Heron Ho. TA6: B'wtr 1A **14**
Hestercombe Cl.
TA6: B'wtr 1B **12**
Hewett Cl. TA1: Taun 4G **27**
Highcroft TA7: Wlvgtn 4G **5**
Higher Palmerston Rd.
TA1: Taun........................5H **21**
Higher Poole TA21: Poole......1G **31**
Higher Rd. TA7: C'zoy 5E **11**
TA7: Wlvgtn 3G **5**
Highfield TA1: Bish H.............1G **27**
TA1: Taun 2E **27**
Highfield Cl. TA1: Taun 2E **27**
Highfield Cres. TA1: Taun 2E **27**
Highgrove TA1: Taun 3A **28**
Highgrove Cl. TA6: B'wtr 3G **13**
Highlands TA1: Taun 3A **28**
High Path TA21: Well 2C **30**
High St. TA1: Taun 1B **28**
TA4: Bish L.......................2B **18**
TA5: Cann..........................2E **7**
TA5: Spax...........................6A **6**
TA6: B'wtr 1F **13**
TA6: N Peth.......................3D **16**
TA21: Well..........................3D **30**
Hilary Rd. TA1: Taun..............1H **27**
Hilda Coles Ho. TA6: B'wtr.....1F **13**
(off Albert St.)
Hillgrove Cl. TA6: B'wtr 6E **9**
Hill Head Cl. TA1: Taun..........1C **28**
Hillsboro TA7: Wlvgtn..............4H **5**
Hillside TA7: P'ton 4C **4**
Hillside Cres. TA7: P'ton 4C **4**
Hillside Dr. TA7: P'ton 4C **4**
Hillside Gro. TA1: Taun..........2G **27**
Hill Ter. TA1: Bish H 6E **21**
Hillyfields TA1: Taun 2E **29**
Hilly Head TA21: Well 4B **30**
Hilly Pk. TA2: Nort F 3C **20**
Hine Rd. TA1: Taun..................3F **27**
Hinton Dr. TA1: Taun 3A **28**
Hither Mead TA4: Bish L.........3B **18**
Hobbs Mead TA4: Bish L.........3C **18**
Holford Rd. TA2: Taun.............2A **22**
TA6: B'wtr 1A **12**
Hollow La. TA6: Wemb 5C **8**
Holly Cl. TA1: Taun..................3E **29**
TA6: B'wtr 6C **10**
TA6: N Peth 3E **17**
Holway 2E 29
Holway TA6: N Peth 2F **17**
Holway Av. TA1: Taun..............1C **28**
Holway Deane TA1: Taun.........2F **29**
Holway Grn. TA1: Taun............2E **29**
Holway Hill TA1: Taun..............1D **28**
Holway Rd. TA1: Taun...............1D **28**
Holyoake St. TA21: Well 2C **30**
Homberg Way
TA6: B'wtr, Wemb 6D **8**
Homecastle Ho. TA6: B'wtr......6F **9**
Home Cotts. TA1: Taun 5H **21**
(off Roseberry Ter.)
Homefield TA21: Well..............5E **31**
Homefield Cl.
TA3: Creech M...................4C **24**
Honiton Rd. TA3: Trull.............6G **27**
Hoopers Cl. TA1: Taun.............2F **27**
Hope Corner Cl.
TA2: Taun 2A **22**
Hope Corner La.
TA2: Taun 2A **22**
Hornbeam Cl. TA1: Taun 2F **29**
TA6: B'wtr 6B **10**
Horner Rd. TA2: Taun 3D **22**
Horsepond La. TA6: B'wtr 1F **13**
Horsey 2C 10
Horsey La.
TA6: B'wtr, H'sey 1A **10**
(in three parts)
TA7: H'sey 1B **10**
(in two parts)
Horton Way TA7: Wlvgtn...........4G **5**
Horts Rd. TA1: Taun.................3G **27**
Hoveland Cres. TA1: Taun 2H **27**
Hoveland Dr. TA1: Taun 3H **27**
Hoveland La. TA1: Taun...........2G **27**
Hovelands Ct. TA1: Taun.........2H **27**
Howard Rd. TA21: Well.............2D **30**
Howell's La. TA6: Thurlo 6B **16**
Hoyles Cl. TA21: Well...............5E **31**
Hoyles Rd. TA21: Well..............5E **31**
Hudson Way TA2: Taun............4F **21**
Hughes Cl. TA6: B'wtr 1H **13**
Hugo St. TA1: Taun 6C **22**
Huish Cl. TA1: Taun 6F **23**
Hulkshay La. TA6: N Peth 3C **16**
Humber Gro. TA1: Taun............1F **29**
Humphreys St. TA21: Well 2E **31**
Huntworth 6A 14
Huntworth Bus. Pk.
TA6: B'wtr 5H **13**
Huntworth La. TA6: N Peth.......1F **17**
TA7: Hunt...........................1G **17**
Hurdle Way TA1: Taun..............1C **28**
Hyacinth Ter. TA21: Well..........4C **30**
Hyde La. TA2: B'pool 4G **23**
TA3: Creech M....................3A **24**
Hyde La. Cotts.
TA2: B'pool.........................3A **24**
Hyde La. Pk. TA2: B'pool..........4G **23**
Hyde Pk. TA6: N Peth...............3D **16**
Hyde Pk. Av. TA6: N Peth 3D **16**
Hylton Cl. TA2: Taun 2B **22**

I

Ilford Ct. TA1: Taun 2G **27**
(off Wiltshire Cl.)
Ilminster Rd. TA1: Taun.............6F **23**
Immenstadt Dr.
TA21: Well...........................5D **30**
Improvement Pl.
TA21: Well...........................4D **30**
(off Bulford La.)
Inner Circ. TA1: Taun................5F **23**
Inner Gullands TA1: Taun 1H **27**
Inwood Rd. TA6: Wemb 6C **8**
Irene Cl. TA6: B'wtr...................4B **10**
Irvine Cl. TA2: Taun 4G **21**
Irwell Grn. TA1: Taun 6F **23**
Ivors Way TA6: N Peth 2D **16**
Ivy Gro. Cl. TA6: B'wtr 4B **10**
Ivy Ho. TA21: Well.......................3C **30**

J

Janson Cl. TA6: B'wtr...............5B **10**
Japonica Cl. TA6: B'wtr 6B **10**
Jarmyns TA1: Bish H 1E **27**
Jeffreys Way TA1: Taun 2D **26**
Jellalabad Ct. TA1: Taun............1B **28**
John Grinter Way
TA21: Well...........................5D **30**
Jubilee Cl. TA6: B'wtr 1A **14**
Jubilee St. TA2: Taun 4A **22**
Judy's Orchard
TA7: W'land.........................2G **15**
Juniper Cl. TA6: B'wtr................1C **14**
Juniper Rd. TA1: Taun................2E **29**
Jurston La. TA21: Well 3E **31**
(in three parts)

K

Keats Rd. TA1: Taun...................1E **29**
Keltings TA6: Wemb....................5C **8**
Kelway Rd. TA21: Well................2E **31**
Kendale Rd. TA6: B'wtr 6E **9**
Kendall Cl. TA3: Creech H 1D **24**
Kennet Gro. TA1: Taun...............6F **23**
Kensington Gdns.
TA6: B'wtr 5B **10**
Kent Av. TA6: B'wtr 3G **13**
Kenwyn Cl. TA1: Taun.................1F **29**
Kestrel Cl. TA6: B'wtr.................2A **14**
Kidsbury Rd. TA6: B'wtr 5E **9**
Kilburn Dr. TA6: B'wtr 5B **10**
Kilkenny Av. TA2: Taun................4B **22**
Kilkenny Ct. TA2: Taun................4B **22**
Killams Av. TA1: Taun.................5D **28**
Killams Cl. TA1: Taun 4D **28**
Killams Cres. TA1: Taun 4D **28**
Killams Dr. TA1: Taun 4D **28**
Killams Grn. TA1: Taun...............4D **28**
Killams La. TA1: Taun.................4D **28**
TA3: Shore 6C **28**
Kilmorie Cl. TA1: Taun................2G **27**
Kilve Cl. TA2: Taun.....................3B **22**
Kilve Cres. TA2: Taun.................3B **22**
Kimberley Ter. TA6: B'wtr 4H **9**
Kinders Cl. TA7: Wlvgtn..............4H **5**
King Alfred Cl.
TA6: N Peth 2E **17**
Kingdom La. TA2: Nort F 4D **20**
Kingdon Mead
TA3: Creech M......................4C **24**
Kingfisher Cl. TA6: B'wtr 2A **14**
King George Av. TA6: B'wtr 3F **13**
King's Castle Bus. Est.
TA6: B'wtr 5G **9**
Kingscliffe Ter. TA6: B'wtr 3G **13**
Kings Cl. TA1: Taun 2C **28**
Kingsdown Cl. TA6: B'wtr 5B **10**
Kings Dr. TA7: W'land 5H **15**
Kingsley Cl. TA1: Taun..............3G **27**
King's Pl. TA6: B'wtr..................6F **9**
King Sq. TA6: B'wtr 6F **9**
Kingston Cl. TA2: Taun..............3A **22**
Kingston Rd. TA2:
Nails, Staple, Taun 1A **22**
King St. TA6: B'wtr 6F **9**
Kingsway TA1: Taun..................4D **28**
Kirk Dr. TA7: W'land..................4H **15**
Kirke Gro. TA2: Taun.................2D **22**
Kitchener Rd. TA2: Nort F.........1B **20**
Kitts TA21: Well.........................5D **30**
Knapp 4H 25
Knapp Rd. TA3: N Curry.............5G **25**
Knightsbridge Way
TA6: B'wtr 5B **10**
Knights Rd. TA21: C'ston 2H **31**
Knoll Grn. La. TA5: Cann 2A **6**
Knowle 1F 11
Knowle End TA7: Wlvgtn............5H **5**
Knowle Rd. TA6: B'wtr 5A **10**

L

Laburnum Cl. TA6: B'wtr..........1B **14**
Laburnum Ct. TA1: Taun 6C **22**
(off Laburnum St.)
Laburnum Rd. TA21: Well 4E **31**
Laburnum St. TA1: Taun 6C **22**
Laburnum Ter.
TA3: Creech M.....................4C **24**
La Ciotat Ho. TA6: B'wtr 1G **13**
Ladylawn TA3: Trull..................5H **27**
Ladymead Cl. TA6: B'wtr 1B **12**
Ladymead Rd. TA2: Taun..........1B **22**
Lakeside Pk. TA6: B'wtr.............2G **13**
Lamb La. TA6: B'wtr....................1F **13**
Lambrook Cl. TA1: Taun 6D **22**
Lambrook Rd. TA1: Taun 5D **22**
Lambrook Way TA1: Taun..........6E **23**
Lancock St. TA21: R Grn...........4A **30**
Langaller 2B 24
Langaller La. TA2: B'pool,
Creech M, Lang....................1A **24**
TA3: Creech M......................1A **24**
Langford 2D 20
Langford La. TA2: Nort F 2D **20**
Langham Dr. TA1: Taun 3G **27**
Langham Gdns. TA1: Taun.......3G **27**
Langmoor Drove
TA7: W'land.........................3H **15**
Lansdowne Rd. TA2: Taun 4C **22**
Larch Cl. TA1: Taun 2F **29**
TA6: B'wtr 5B **10**
Larkspur Cl. TA1: Taun...............3E **29**
Larkspur Ct. TA2: Taun 3H **21**
Laurel Cl. TA1: Taun...................2E **29**
Laurels, The TA6: Wemb 5C **8**
Lavender Gro. TA1: Bish H 1G **27**
Laverock Ct. TA1: Taun...............5A **22**
Lawn Mdw. TA3: Ruish 6B **24**
Lawn Rd. TA2: Staple...................2G **21**
Laxton Cl. TA1: Taun 5F **23**
Laxton Rd. TA1: Taun 5F **23**
Leadon Gro. TA1: Taun...............1F **29**
Leafield Cl. TA2: Nort F 3C **20**
Leat, The TA4: Bish L...................3C **18**
Leeward Cl. TA6: B'wtr 1A **14**
Leggar, The TA6: B'wtr 6G **9**
Leigh Rd. TA2: Taun 2D **22**
Leonard Houlder Ct.
TA2: Taun 2C **22**
Leslie Av. TA2: Taun...................4A **22**
Lethbridge Pk. TA4: Bish L 2A **18**
Lewis Rd. TA2: Taun...................3A **22**
Leycroft Cl. TA1: Taun................6D **22**
Leycroft Gro. TA1: Taun 6D **22**
Leycroft Rd. TA1: Taun 6D **22**
Leyton Dr. TA6: B'wtr 5B **10**
Liberty Pl. TA6: B'wtr.................1H **13**
Lilac Cl. TA1: Taun 2E **29**
Lillebonne Cl. TA21: Well 3E **31**
Lime Cres. TA1: Taun.................2E **29**
Limestone Hill TA5: Cann..........4G **7**
Lime Tree Cl. TA6: B'wtr............1B **14**
Linden Cl. TA6: B'wtr 1A **14**
Linden Gro. TA1: Taun 5A **22**
Linden Hill TA21: West 3A **30**
Lindsey Cres. TA6: N Peth 3E **17**
Liney 1H 15
Liney Rd. TA7: W'land 1H **15**
Linham Rd. TA6: B'wtr 5F **9**
Linley Cl. TA6: B'wtr 4B **10**
Linnet Cl. TA1: Bish H 6F **21**
Lipe Hill La. TA4: Comey............6C **26**
TA21: Comey, W Buck.......6C **26**
Lipe La. TA3: H'lade, Ruish.......6B **24**
Lisieux Ct. TA1: Taun..................2F **29**
Lisieux Way TA1: Taun...............6E **23**
Little Cl. TA2: Staple...................2G **21**
Little Mdw. TA4: Bish L...............3C **18**
Lit. Silver La. TA21: Well 6D **30**
Lit. Wall La.
TA7: B'drip, Kwle..................1F **11**
Livingstone Way TA2: Taun 4F **21**
Lloyd Cl. TA1: Taun 3F **27**
Load La. TA7: W'land...................5H **15**
Lockswell TA7: Wlvgtn.................3H **5**
Lodge Cl. TA1: Taun 2E **27**
TA21: Well..........................3D **30**
Longacre Cl. TA2: Taun...............3A **22**
Longacre Drove TA7: C'zoy 1E **15**
Longforth Rd. TA21: Well...........2D **30**
Long La. TA2: Lang......................1C **24**
Longmead Cl. TA1: Taun............2H **27**
TA21: Tone..........................1B **30**
Longmead Way TA1: Taun 2H **27**
Longrun La. TA1: Bish H.............5G **21**
Longstone Av. TA6: B'wtr...........1A **14**
Lonsdale Rd. TA5: Cann..............2F **7**
Lords Way TA6: B'wtr...................5E **9**
Lovers' Wlk. TA5: Cann..............2E **7**
Lwr. Bath Rd. TA6: B'wtr 5H **9**
Lwr. Foxmoor Rd.
TA21: R Grn 4B **30**
Lwr. Holway Cl. TA1: Taun 2F **29**
Lwr. Middle St. TA1: Taun 6B **22**
Lower Rd. TA7: Wlvgtn................3G **5**
Lower Westford 3A 30
Lowlands Ter. TA1: Bish H 6F **21**
Lowmoor Ind. Est.
TA21: Tone..........................1B **30**
Loxleigh Av. TA6: B'wtr..............1H **13**
Loxleigh Gdns. TA6: B'wtr........1H **13**
Loxley Ter. TA6: B'wtr..................4F **9**
Ludlow Av. TA2: Taun.................2C **22**
Ludlow Cl. TA6: B'wtr 3G **13**
Luttrell Cl. TA2: Taun.................2D **22**
Luxborough Rd. TA6: B'wtr 1A **12**
Luxhay Cl. TA2: Taun 2D **22**
Lyddon Cl. TA21: Well.................5D **30**
Lydeard Mead TA4: Bish L 3B **18**
Lyndale Av. TA6: B'wtr 6E **9**
Lyndhurst Cres. TA6: Wemb 6C **8**
Lyngford 4C 22
Lyngford Cres. TA2: Taun...........3C **22**
Lyngford La.
TA2: Ched F, Taun................2C **22**
Lyngford Pl. TA2: Taun...............3C **22**
Lyngford Rd. TA2: Taun..............4C **22**
Lyngford Sq. TA2: Taun...............3C **22**
Lynor Cl. TA1: Taun 1F **29**

M

Maddocks Ct. TA6: B'wtr 5F **9**
(off Waverley Wharf)
Magdalene La. TA1: Taun.........6B **22**

Magdalene St. TA1: Taun......6B **22**
Magnolia Tree Rd.
  TA6: B'wtr 6C **10**
Maidenbrook La.
  TA2: Ched F 1E **23**
Main Rd. TA5: Cann 2F **7**
  TA7: W'land.....................2G **15**
Mallard Way TA6: B'wtr 1G **13**
Mallory Cl. TA2: Taun...........4F **21**
Malthouse Ct. TA1: Bish H ...6E **21**
Malvern Cl. TA6: B'wtr 5B **10**
Malvern Ter. TA2: Taun........4B **22**
Mandarin Cl. TA6: B'wtr 1H **13**
Manning Rd. TA4: Cotf L 6A **18**
Manor Cl. TA1: Taun 2A **28**
Manor Dr. TA1: Taun 1A **28**
  TA2: Staple......................3G **21**
  TA7: C'zoy........................5F **11**
Manor M. TA2: Staple 2H **21**
Manor Orchard TA1: Taun ...2H **27**
  TA2: Staple......................2G **21**
Manor Pk. TA2: Nort F........4C **20**
Manor Rd. TA1: Taun 1H **27**
  TA2: Staple......................3G **21**
  TA6: B'wtr 5A **10**
  TA7: C'zoy........................5F **11**
Manse La. TA7: P'ton...........4C **4**
Mansfield Rd. TA1: Taun......1C **28**
Mansion Ho. La. TA6: B'wtr 6F **9**
  (off High St.)
Mantle St. TA21: Well 4C **30**
Maple Cl. TA2: Taun 3C **22**
  TA6: N Peth 3E **17**
  TA7: P'ton........................4C **4**
Maple Ct. TA6: B'wtr............5B **10**
March La. TA7: B'drip 2E **11**
Marden Gro. TA1: Taun 1F **29**
Marina Row TA6: B'wtr.......1H **13**
Mariners Cl. TA6: B'wtr 6G **9**
Mariners Ct. TA6: B'wtr 6G **9**
  (off Mariners Cl.)
Market Ct. TA6: B'wtr............6F **9**
  (off Market St.)
Market St. TA6: B'wtr............6F **9**
Marks Cl. TA3: Ruish 5A **24**
Marlborough Av.
  TA6: B'wtr 3G **13**
Marlborough Cl.
  TA6: B'wtr 3G **13**
Marshalsea Wlk.
  TA1: Taun 6A **22**
Marsh La. TA5: Cann 1G **7**
Marston Cl. TA1: Taun.........3A **28**
Martins TA3: Ruish 6A **24**
Martins Cl. TA21: Well.........4D **30**
Martland Cl. TA7: Wlvgtn.....5H **5**
Mary St. TA1: Taun 1B **28**
Matthews Rd. TA1: Taun......3F **27**
Maunsel Rd. TA7: N New 6F **17**
Maxwell St. TA2: Taun 4A **22**
Mayfield Dr. TA6: B'wtr.......1B **12**
Mayflower Cl. TA6: B'wtr......6B **10**
McCreath Cl. TA6: N Peth 3E **17**
Meade Cl. TA6: N Peth 3E **17**
Meadow Cl. TA5: Chil T 2F **9**
Meadowlands Av.
  TA6: B'wtr, Wemb.............5E **9**
Meadow Pk. TA6: Wemb......6C **8**
Meadowside TA21: R Grn 4B **30**
Meadowside Cl.
  TA1: Bish H......................6F **21**
Meads Cl. TA6: B'wtr 2E **13**
Meads Droveway
  TA3: Creech M.................2D **24**
Meadway TA2: Monk H 1G **23**
  TA7: Wlvgtn......................4G **5**
Medway Cl. TA1: Taun.........6F **23**
Melbourne Pl. TA6: B'wtr.....5H **9**
Melcombe La. TA6: N Peth 2C **16**
Mendip Rd. TA6: B'wtr 1A **14**
Merle Cl. TA6: B'wtr 1H **13**
Merridge Cl. TA6: B'wtr 1A **12**
Merryfields TA4: Cotf L 5A **18**
Middle Drove TA5: Chil T......1D **8**
Middle Green 6E **31**
Middle Grn. Rd.
  TA21: Well 5E **31**
Middle Moore Drove
  TA7: Wlvgtn......................1H **5**
Middlemoor Water Pk. 2H **5**

Middlestream Cl.
  TA6: B'wtr..........................3D **12**
Middle St. TA1: Taun...........6B **22**
  TA7: P'ton.........................3C **4**
Middleway TA1: Taun...........3A **28**
Midford Rd. TA1: Taun..........1D **28**
Milestone Cl. TA6: N Peth.....2E **17**
Milford Pl. TA1: Taun............6C **22**
  (off Winchester St.)
Millbay TA6: N Peth 2D **16**
Mill Cl. TA5: Cann 2F **7**
Mill Cotts. TA3: Creech M.....5C **24**
Millers Way TA4: Bish L 3B **18**
Mill Farm Hill
  TA5: Cann, Charl 4B **6**
Mill La. TA1: Taun 6B **22**
  TA3: Creech M.................5C **24**
  TA3: Trull 5H **27**
  TA4: Bish L 3B **18**
  TA5: Cann 2F **7**
Mill La. Cl. TA3: Trull 5H **27**
Mill Ri. TA2: Staple 3F **21**
Mill Stream Gdns.
  TA21: Tone 1B **30**
Mill St. TA6: N Peth 3E **17**
  TA7: Wlvgtn......................5H **5**
Millwood Cl. TA6: B'wtr.......3E **13**
Milne Cl. TA6: B'wtr 3F **13**
Milton Cl. TA1: Taun 1E **29**
Milton Dr. TA1: Taun 1E **29**
Milton Hill TA2: Monk H 2G **23**
Milton Pl. TA1: Taun 1E **13**
Milton Rd. TA1: Taun 1D **28**
Milverton Rd.
  TA21: R'ton, Tone............1A **30**
Minehead Rd. TA4: Bish L 3B **18**
Minster Cl. TA1: Taun 3G **27**
Minster Ct. TA1: Taun 3G **27**
Mitchell St. TA21: Well 2C **30**
Mitre Ct. TA1: Taun 6D **22**
Monks Cl. TA1: Taun 5D **22**
Monkton Heathfield 2G **23**
Monmouth Cl.
  TA7: W'land......................1G **15**
Monmouth Rd. TA1: Taun.....5D **22**
  TA7: W'land......................1G **15**
Monmouth St. TA6: B'wtr....6G **9**
Montys La. TA4: Nort F........2A **20**
Monument Cl. TA21: Well 5E **31**
Monument Rd. TA21: Well 5E **31**
Moonraker Cl. TA6: B'wtr.....1H **13**
Moor Drove TA7: C'zoy........5H **11**
Moore's La. TA5: Wemb 4B **8**
Moorhaven Cl. TA1: Taun 1E **29**
Moorland Cl. TA1: Taun........5E **23**
Moorland Pl. TA1: Taun........5E **23**
Moorland Rd. TA1: Taun 5E **23**
  TA6: B'wtr 1A **14**
Moorlands TA4: Bish L 3C **18**
Moorland Way TA6: B'wtr.....6B **10**
Moormead Drove
  TA7: Wlvgtn......................1G **5**
Moots La. TA6: B'wtr 1A **14**
Moravia Cl. TA6: B'wtr 5E **9**
Morgans Ri. TA1: Bish H......1E **29**
Mornington Pk. TA21: Well ...4E **31**
Mortimer Cl. TA7: Wlvgtn.....3H **5**
Moss Cl. TA6: B'wtr 5A **10**
Moss La. TA3: Ruish 6A **24**
Mountbatten Ho. TA6: B'wtr...6A **10**
  (off Parkway)
Mountfields Av. TA1: Taun....3D **28**
Mountfields Pk. TA1: Taun....3D **28**
Mountfields Rd. TA1: Taun ...4C **28**
Mount La. TA1: Taun 1C **28**
Mount Nebo TA1: Taun 2A **28**
Mount St. TA1: Taun 1B **28**
  TA4: Bish L 2B **18**
  TA6: B'wtr 6F **9**
Mount Ter. TA1: Taun 1C **28**
Mount, The TA1: Taun 1B **28**
Mount Vw. TA7: Wlvgtn.......4H **5**
Mount Wlk. TA1: Taun 1C **28**
Mountway Cl. TA1: Bish H 6G **21**
Mountway Rd. TA1: Bish H ...6F **21**
Mulberry Cl. TA1: Taun.........2E **29**
Mulberry Tree Cl.
  TA6: B'wtr 6B **10**

MUSGROVE PARK HOSPITAL
  ....1G **27**
Musgrove Rd. TA1: Taun.......1G **27**
Myrtle Cl. TA6: B'wtr............6B **10**

N

Naples Vw. TA6: Wemb........4E **9**
Nash Grn. TA2: Staple 3F **21**
Needhams Patch
  TA4: Cotf L 6A **18**
Nelson Ct. TA6: B'wtr 6F **9**
  (off Drakes Cl.)
Nerrols Dr. TA2: Taun............2D **22**
Netherclay TA1: Bish H..........6F **21**
Newbarn Rd. TA1: Taun.........3F **27**
New Bldgs. TA7: D'wear......4B **14**
Newlands Cres.
  TA3: Ruish 6B **24**
Newlands Gro. TA3: Ruish....6B **24**
Newlands Rd. TA3: Ruish 6A **24**
New La. TA2: Lang 2B **24**
Newlyn Cres. TA7: P'ton 3B **4**
New Rd. TA3: Trull 4G **27**
  TA5: Cann 4G **7**
  TA6: B'wtr 6G **9**
  TA7: B'drip, Kwle..............1F **11**
Newton Rd. TA1: Taun 6G **23**
  TA6: N Peth 3D **16**
Newtown 5E **9**
Nicholls Cl. TA6: B'wtr..........1D **12**
Nichol Pl. TA4: Cotf L 6B **18**
Nightingale Cl. TA6: B'wtr 1A **14**
Nightingale Ct. TA1: Taun 6C **22**
Nightingales TA4: Cotf L 6A **18**
Noble St. TA1: Taun 6D **22**
Norfolk Cl. TA6: B'wtr 2A **14**
Normandy Dr. TA1: Taun 1E **29**
Northbrook Rd. TA5: Cann 2G **7**
North End 3C **24**
North End TA3: Creech M 3C **24**
Northern Distributor Rd.
  TA6: B'wtr.........................4F **9**
  (nr. Chilton Rd.)
  TA6: B'wtr.........................6D **8**
  (nr. Quantock Rd.)
Northfield 1E **13**
Northfield TA6: B'wtr 1E **13**
Northfield Av. TA1: Taun 6A **22**
Northfield Gdns. TA1: Taun....6A **22**
  (in two parts)
Northfield Rd. TA1: Taun.......5A **22**
  (in two parts)
Northfields TA1: Bish H 6F **21**
Northgate TA6: B'wtr 6F **9**
Northleigh Rd. TA1: Taun......1D **28**
Nth. Mead Drove TA7: P'ton ...1C **4**
Northmoor Drove
  TA7: B'drip........................3F **11**
North Newton 6F **17**
North Petherton 2D **16**
Northside TA21: R Grn 4B **30**
North St. TA1: Taun 6B **22**
  TA6: B'wtr 6E **9**
  TA6: N Peth 2D **16**
  TA21: Well.........................3D **30**
North Town 5A **22**
North Vs. TA4: Cotf L 6B **18**
Northwood Cl. TA2: Nort F....4D **20**
Norton Fitzwarren 4D **20**
Norwich Cl. TA1: Taun 3G **27**
Norwich Ct. TA1: Taun 2H **27**
Nowers La. TA1: Well 6C **30**
Nunsfield Ct. TA1: Taun 1C **28**
  (in two parts)
Nursery Ter. TA6: B'wtr........6E **9**
Nynehead Rd. TA21: Poole 1E **31**

O

Oak Apple Dr. TA6: Wemb 5D **8**
Oakenford La. TA5: Goat......6A **12**
Oaken Ground TA21: R Grn....4B **30**
  (in two parts)
Oakfield Pk. TA21: Well 5E **31**
Oakfield Rd. TA6: B'wtr 2C **12**
Oakgrove Way TA1: Taun 4B **10**
Oakley Cl. TA7: W'land 2G **15**

Oaks, The TA1: Taun 3E **29**
  TA6: Wemb 5C **8**
Oak Tree Way TA5: Cann 2F **7**
Oatley La. TA5: Cann 1A **6**
Obridge 4C **22**
Obridge Cl. TA2: Taun...........4C **22**
Obridge Cres. TA2: Taun.......5C **22**
Obridge La. TA2: Taun 5C **22**
Obridge Rd. TA2: Taun..........4C **22**
Obridge Viaduct TA1: Taun ...5D **22**
Obridge Wlk. TA2: Taun........5B **22**
Octagon, The TA1: Taun........6B **22**
Olands Rd. TA21: Well...........3D **30**
Old Basin TA6: B'wtr.............3H **13**
Old Broach La. TA3: H'don 2H **29**
Old Comeytrowe La.
  TA1: Taun..........................3F **27**
Old Mkt. Cen. TA1: Taun 1B **28**
Old Mill Rd. TA7: Wlvgtn.......5H **5**
Old Oaks Cl. TA6: Wemb 6D **8**
Old Rd. TA6: N Peth 2E **17**
Old Taunton Rd. TA6: B'wtr ...1G **13**
Old Vicarage La.
  TA4: Bish L 2B **18**
Oldway Pk. TA21: Well 5F **31**
Oldway Rd. TA21: Well 6C **30**
Orchard Cl. TA3: Trull 5G **27**
  TA6: N Peth 3D **16**
  TA21: West.........................4A **30**
Orchard Ct. TA21: Well 3E **31**
Orchard Dr. TA1: Bish H 1E **27**
Orchard Grn. TA2: Taun 2B **22**
Orchard La. TA6: Wemb 6D **8**
Orchard Portman 6E **29**
Orchard Ri. TA3: Ruish 5A **24**
Orchard Way TA1: Taun 1A **28**
  TA7: Wlvgtn.......................5H **5**
Orchid Cl. TA1: Taun 4E **29**
Osborne Gro. TA1: Taun 1A **28**
Osborne Rd. TA6: B'wtr 5F **9**
Osborne Way TA1: Taun 1A **28**
Outer Circ. TA1: Taun 5F **23**
Outer Gullands TA1: Taun.....2H **27**
Overlands TA3: Ruish............5B **24**
Owen St. TA21: Well 3C **30**
Oxford Pl. TA2: Taun 2C **22**
Oxford Ter. TA6: B'wtr...........1H **13**
Oxleaze TA4: Bish L 3C **18**

P

Paddock Cl.
  TA3: Creech M...................3C **24**
Paddocks, The TA21: Well......4E **31**
Paddock, The TA21: Well 4D **28**
  TA3: Trull 4H **27**
Palmer Cl. TA6: B'wtr 3F **13**
Palmerston Rd. TA1: Taun 5H **21**
Palm Tree Cl. TA6: B'wtr.......6C **10**
Parchey 5H **11**
Park Av. TA6: B'wtr 1D **12**
Park Cl. TA3: Trull 6H **27**
Parker Cl. TA21: Well 3E **31**
Parkfield Cl. TA6: N Peth.......2F **17**
Parkfield Cres. TA1: Taun 1H **27**
Parkfield Dr. TA1: Taun 1G **27**
Parkfield Rd. TA1: Taun 1H **27**
Parkfield Wlk. TA1: Taun 2H **27**
Parklands TA21: Well............2D **30**
Park La. TA5: Cann 1E **7**
  TA5: Goat, N Peth..............1A **16**
  TA6: N Peth 2A **16**
  (nr. Dancing Hill)
  TA6: N Peth 1F **17**
  (nr. Taunton Rd.)
  TA7: N Peth 2G **17**
  TA21: C'ston......................2H **31**
Park Mead TA2: Monk H 2G **23**
Park Rd. TA6: B'wtr 1D **12**
Parkside Ct. TA6: B'wtr.........1H **13**
Parks, The TA6: B'wtr 1E **13**
Parkstone Av. TA6: B'wtr 3F **13**
Park St. TA1: Taun................1A **28**
Pk. Wall Drove TA7: C'zoy.....5D **10**
  (nr. Chedzoy La.)
  TA7: C'zoy..........................1D **14**
  (nr. Portwall Drove)
Park Way TA3: Ruish 6A **24**
Parkway TA6: B'wtr 1A **14**

Parmin Cl. TA1: Taun 1E 29
Parmin Way TA1: Taun 1E 29
Parrett Mead TA1: Taun 1F 29
Parsonage Ct. TA1: Bish H....6E 21
  TA7: P'ton 3B 4
Pathfinder Ter. TA6: B'wtr ...1H 13
  (off Colley La.)
Patrick's Way TA3: Trull 6G 27
Patrum Cl. TA1: Taun 3F 27
Paul St. TA1: Taun 1B 28
  (in two parts)
Pawlett Mead Drove TA6: P'lett1A 4
Pawlett Rd. TA7: P'ton 2A 4
Payton Rd. TA21: West 3A 30
Peace Cl. TA6: B'wtr 5B 10
Peach Tree Cl. TA6: B'wtr 6C 10
Pear Tree Cl. TA6: B'wtr 1B 14
Peile Dr. TA1: Taun 3A 22
Pelham Ct. TA6: B'wtr 5B 10
Pembroke Cl. TA1: Taun 3G 27
Pembroke Rd. TA6: B'wtr.....2A 14
Penarth Rd. TA6: B'wtr 1D 12
Pen Elm 1C 20
Pen Elm Hill TA2: Nort F 1C 20
Penel Orlieu TA6: B'wtr 1F 13
Penlea Av. TA6: B'wtr 3E 13
Penlea Cl. TA6: B'wtr 3E 13
Penny Cl. TA21: Well 2D 30
Penzoy Av. TA1: Taun 1H 13
Penzoy Drove TA7: W'land....4H 15
Perry Green 3A 8
Peter St. TA2: Taun 4B 22
Petherton Rd. TA7: N New.....5F 17
Petrel Cl. TA6: B'wtr 4B 10
Phillip Ho. TA1: Taun 3F 13
Phillips Cl. TA6: B'wtr 1D 12
Phoenix Rd. TA6: B'wtr 2H 13
Pickeridge Cl. TA2: Taun 3C 22
Pickney 3G 19
Pickney La. TA2: King M.......3G 19
Piffin La. TA4: Bish L 2B 18
Pig La. TA7: C'zoy 5F 11
Pig Mkt. La. TA1: Taun 1B 28
Pikes Cres. TA1: Taun 3A 28
Pilots Helm TA6: N Peth 2D 16
  (in two parts)
Pine Cl. TA1: Taun 2F 29
Pinetree Cl. TA6: B'wtr 6B 10
Pinney Cl. TA1: Taun 3F 27
Pippins, The TA6: Wemb 5D 8
Pitts Cl. TA1: Taun 2G 27
Plais St. TA2: Taun 4B 22
Pleamore Cross 6A 30
Plum La. TA6: D'wear 3A 14
Plum Tree Cl. TA6: B'wtr......6C 10
Polden St. TA6: B'wtr 6G 9
Polden Wlk. TA7: Wlvgtn......5G 5
Pollard Rd. TA6: B'wtr 5B 10
Pollards Way TA1: Taun 6A 22
Pool Cl. TA7: P'ton 3C 4
Poole 1F 31
Pope Cl. TA1: Taun 4G 27
Pope's La.
  TA21: B Grn, R Grn 5B 30
Popham Cl. TA6: B'wtr 6B 10
Popham Flats TA21: Well.....3D 30
  (off Victoria St.)
Poplar Rd. TA1: Taun 2F 29
  TA6: B'wtr 5B 10
Porlock Dr. TA1: Taun 3A 28
Portland Cl. TA5: Cann 1F 7
Portland Grange TA1: Taun ...1A 28
Portland Pl. TA1: Taun 6A 22
  TA6: B'wtr 6D 8
Portland St. TA1: Taun 6A 22
Portman Cres. TA6: N Peth....4D 16
Portman Dr. TA6: N Peth.......4D 16
Portman Rd. TA6: N Peth......4D 16
  (in two parts)
Portman St. TA1: Taun 1B 28
Portwall Drove TA7: C'zoy 6D 10
Positano Ct. TA6: Wemb 4E 9
Poskitt Ho. TA6: B'wtr 5F 9
  (off Waverley Rd.)
Post Cl. TA21: Well 5E 31
Potterton Cl. TA6: B'wtr 3F 13
Poundfield TA6: B'wtr 4F 9
Poundfield La. TA3: Durs 1H 25
Poundisford Cl. TA1: Taun ...3H 27

Pound La. TA4: Bish L 2C 18
Powell Cl. TA3: Creech M 4C 24
Princess Cl. TA6: N Peth 2E 17
Princes St. TA1: Taun 6D 22
Priors Wlk. TA1: Taun 6B 22
Priorswood 3C 22
Priorswood Ind. Est.
  TA2: Taun 4E 23
Priorswood Pl. TA2: Taun 3C 22
Priorswood Rd. TA2: Taun 4B 22
  (in two parts)
Priory TA21: Well 3E 31
Priory Av. TA2: Taun 6B 22
  (in two parts)
Priory Bri. Rd. TA1: Taun 5B 22
Priory Cl. TA5: Cann 2G 7
Priory Ct. TA1: Taun 6C 22
  TA6: B'wtr 1F 13
  TA21: Well 2E 31
Priory Flds. TA1: Taun 5C 22
Priory Gdns. TA21: Well 3E 31
Priory, The TA21: Well 3E 31
Priory Way TA1: Taun 5D 22
Priory Way Ind. Est.
  TA1: Taun 5D 22
Private Rd. TA2: Taun 3H 21
Prospect Ter. TA1: Taun 5B 22
Provident Pl. TA6: B'wtr........6E 9
Prowses Mdw. TA2: Nort F ...4D 20
Purewell TA7: P'ton 3C 4
Puriton 3C 4
Puriton Hill
  TA7: Kwle, P'ton 4B 4
  (in two parts)
Puriton Pk. TA7: P'ton..........4C 4
Puriton Rd. TA6: P'lett 2A 4
Purley Dr. TA6: B'wtr 5B 10
Pyles Thorne TA21: Well 5E 31
Pyles Thorne Cl.
  TA21: Well 4E 31
Pyles Thorne Rd.
  TA21: Well 4E 31
Pyrland 1D 22
Pyrland Av. TA2: Taun 2B 22
Pyrland Pl. TA2: Taun 2B 22
Pyrland Wlk. TA6: B'wtr 1A 12

Q

Quantock Av. TA6: B'wtr 1D 12
Quantock Cl. TA6: N Peth 2D 16
Quantock Ho. TA6: N Peth 2D 16
  (off Quantock Cl.)
Quantock Mdw. TA6: B'wtr....6C 8
Quantock Pde.
  TA6: N Peth 2D 16
  (off Quantock Cl.)
Quantock Rd. TA2: Taun 3A 22
  TA5: B'wtr, Wemb 5H 7
  TA6: Wemb 5A 8
  TA21: Well 2D 30
Quantock Ter. TA6: B'wtr 5G 9
Quantock Vw. TA4: Bish L 2B 18
Quantock Way TA6: B'wtr 6C 8
Quayside TA6: B'wtr 6F 9
Queen Elizabeth Ct.
  TA6: B'wtr 6G 9
  (off Blake Pl.)
Queen's Down
  TA3: Creech M...............4B 24
Queens Dr. TA1: Taun 3H 27
Queen's Rd. TA6: B'wtr 3F 13
Queens Rd. TA21: Well 5E 31
Queen St. TA1: Taun 1C 28
  TA6: B'wtr 6F 9
  TA6: N Peth 2E 17
Queensway TA1: Taun 3F 27
Queenswood La.
  TA6: B'wtr 1B 12
Queenswood Rd.
  TA6: B'wtr 1C 12

R

Rackfield TA21: West 4A 30
Radlet Cl. TA2: Taun 3D 22
Raglan Cl. TA6: B'wtr 4A 10

Raglan Ct. TA2: Taun 4B 22
  (off Kilkenny Av.)
Railway St. TA2: Taun 4B 22
Raleigh Cl. TA6: B'wtr 6A 10
Raleigh Ho. TA6: B'wtr 6A 10
  (off Raleigh Cl.)
Ramshorn Cl. TA1: Taun 2G 27
Ramshorn Grn. TA1: Taun 2H 27
Ramshorn Pl. TA1: Taun 2H 27
Raps Cl. TA1: Taun 5G 23
Raps Grn. TA1: Taun 5G 23
Ravello M. TA6: Wemb 4E 9
Raymond St. TA2: Taun 4A 22
Rectory Cl. TA2: Staple 2G 21
  TA6: N Peth 3D 16
Rectory Dr. TA2: Staple 3G 21
Rectory Rd. TA2: Nort F 3C 20
  TA2: Staple 1F 21
Redgate St. TA6: B'wtr 1H 13
Redlake Dr. TA1: Taun 1F 29
Reed Cl. TA6: B'wtr 3F 13
Reedmoor Gdns.
  TA6: Wemb 4E 9
Reeds Dr. TA7: Wlvgtn..........3H 5
Regent Way TA6: B'wtr 3G 13
Rhode 5A 12
Rhode La. TA5:
  Durl, Goat, Rhode 4A 12
  TA6: B'wtr, Rhode 4C 12
Rhodes Cl. TA2: Taun 3F 21
Richards Cl. TA21: Tone 1C 30
Richards Cres.
  TA2: Monk H 1H 23
Richmond Cl. TA6: B'wtr 4F 9
Richmond Grn. TA1: Taun 5H 21
Richmond Pk. TA1: Bish H....6G 21
Richmond Rd. TA1: Taun 5H 21
Ringwood Rd. TA6: B'wtr 3G 13
Risedale Cl. TA6: Wemb 6C 8
Risemoor Rd. TA6: B'wtr 3E 13
River La. TA7: D'wear 3B 14
Riverside TA1: Taun 6A 22
River Vw. TA6: B'wtr 5F 9
Roake La. TA2: Nort F 2C 20
Roberts Dr. TA6: B'wtr 3G 13
Roberts Rd. TA2: Nort F 1B 20
Robin Cl. TA1: Bish H 6F 21
Robins Dr. TA6: B'wtr 5G 9
Rochester Rd. TA2: Taun 2C 22
Rocketts Cl. TA3: Creech M ...4B 24
Rocketts Cotts.
  TA3: Creech M................4B 24
Rockwell Green 4B 30
Rodway 1F 7
Rodway TA5: Cann 1F 7
Roe Cl. TA6: B'wtr 1B 14
Rogers Cl. TA6: N Peth 3E 17
Roland Cl. TA1: Taun 2G 27
Roman La. TA6: B'wtr 2C 12
Roman Rd. TA1: Taun 6E 23
Romney Mead TA1: Taun 1F 29
Rookery Cl. TA7: P'ton..........3C 4
Rookery Ter. TA21: Well........4C 30
Rope Wlk. TA6: B'wtr 6G 9
  TA21: Well 5C 30
Rosary Dr. TA6: B'wtr 1B 12
Roseberry Ter. TA1: Taun 5H 21
Rosebery Av. TA6: B'wtr 6H 9
Rosebery St. TA2: Taun 3A 22
Rose Cotts. TA1: Taun 1D 28
Rosevean Cl. TA6: B'wtr 4B 10
Roughmoor Cl. TA1: Taun 5H 21
Roughmoor Cotts.
  TA1: Taun 5H 21
Roughmoor Cres. TA1: Taun..5H 21
Rowan Cl. TA7: P'ton 4C 4
Rowan Dr. TA1: Taun 3F 29
Rowans Cl. TA6: B'wtr 5A 10
Rowbarton Cl. TA2: Taun 3B 22
Rowe Cl. TA21: R Grn 5A 30
Rowlands Ri. TA7: P'ton........4B 4
Ruborough Rd. TA6: B'wtr 1A 14
Rugg's Drove
  TA7: C'zoy, D'wear 6E 11
Ruishton 6A 24
Ruishton La. TA3: Ruish 6H 23
Ruishton La. Cotts.
  TA3: Ruish 6A 24

Rumwell 3C 26
Runnington 1A 30
Rupert St. TA1: Taun 4A 22
Ruskin Cl. TA1: Taun 1E 29
Russell Pl. TA6: B'wtr 5F 9
Russett Rd. TA1: Taun 5G 23
Ryburn Cl. TA1: Taun 1F 29
Rydon Cres. TA5: Cann.........2F 7
Rydon La. TA2: Taun 2B 22
Rye TA7: P'ton 3C 4
Ryelands Farm Ind. Est.
  TA21: B Grn 6B 30
Ryepool TA4: Bish L 3C 18
Ryesland Way
  TA3: Creech M................4C 24

S

Saffron Cl. TA1: Taun 4D 28
St Albans Pl. TA2: Taun 2B 22
St Andrew's Rd. TA2: Taun 4B 22
St Andrews Vw. TA2: Taun 4A 22
St Anns Cl. TA1: Taun 3A 22
St Augustine St. TA1: Taun ...5C 22
St David's Cl. TA2: Taun 2B 22
St Davids Cl. TA6: B'wtr 1B 14
St George's Av. TA2: Taun 2B 22
St Georges Pl. TA1: Taun 1B 28
St Georges Sq. TA1: Taun 1B 28
St George's Way TA1: Taun ...2A 28
St James Cl. TA1: Taun 6B 22
St James Ct. TA1: Taun 6B 22
  (off St James St.)
  TA6: B'wtr 2B 14
St James St. TA1: Taun 6B 22
St Johns Cl. TA21: Well 3E 31
St John's Rd. TA1: Taun 1A 28
St John St. TA6: B'wtr 6G 9
St Lukes M. TA4: Cotf L 6A 18
St Margarets Ct.
  TA1: Taun 6D 22
ST MARGARET'S SOMERSET
  HOSPICE 6F 21
St Mark's Cl. TA7: C'zoy 5G 11
St Marks Cl. TA6: B'wtr.........2B 14
St Mary's Ct. TA1: Taun 2F 29
  (off Haywood Rd.)
  TA6: B'wtr 1F 13
  TA6: N Peth 2D 16
  (off Watery La.)
St Mary's Cres.
  TA6: N Peth 2E 17
St Mary's Rd. TA7: W'land.....2G 15
St Mary St. TA6: B'wtr 1F 13
St Matthew's Fld.
  TA6: B'wtr 1E 13
St Matthews Grn.
  TA6: B'wtr 1E 13
St Michael Rd.
  TA3: Creech M................4C 24
St Michael's Cl.
  TA3: Creech M................4C 24
St Michaels Ct.
  TA7: B'drip 1G 11
St Michael's Cres.
  TA6: B'wtr 2C 22
St Patrick's Cl. TA2: Taun 2C 22
St Patrick's Rd. TA2: Taun 2C 22
St Pauls Cl. TA6: B'wtr 2B 14
St Peters Cl. TA2: Taun 3C 22
St Peters Cl. TA6: B'wtr 2B 14
St Quintin Pk. TA2: B'pool 4G 23
St Saviour's Av. TA6: B'wtr ...1G 13
St Thomas Cl. TA6: B'wtr 2B 14
Salisbury St. TA2: Taun 4A 22
Salmon Pde. TA6: B'wtr.........6B 22
  (in two parts)
Saltlands TA6: B'wtr 4F 9
Saltlands Av. TA6: B'wtr 4F 9
Saltlands Ho. TA6: B'wtr 4F 9
Samuels Ct. TA1: Taun 4A 22
Sandene Cl. TA2: Staple 2G 21
Sandford Hill TA5: Wemb 4A 8
Sandown Cl. TA6: B'wtr 3G 13
Sandpiper Cl. TA6: B'wtr 1G 13
Sandpiper Rd. TA6: B'wtr 1G 13
Sandringham Cl.
  TA6: B'wtr 4A 10
Sandy La. TA5: Cann 1C 6

Saplings, The. TA1: Taun 2B 28
　(off Wilton Orchard)
Savery Row TA1: Taun 1C 28
Saviano Way TA6: Wemb 4E 9
Savill Dr. TA1: Taun 6E 23
Saxon Grn. TA6: B'wtr 1A 14
Saxon Rd. TA6: B'wtr 1A 14
Scafell Cl. TA1: Taun 3G 27
School Flds. TA5: Cann 2G 7
　TA6: N Peth 3E 17
School La. TA6: N Peth 2E 17
　TA7: Wlvgtn 3H 5
School Rd. TA2: Monk H 2G 23
　TA7: W'land 2G 15
Scott Cl. TA1: Taun 4G 21
Scott's La. TA21: Well 3E 31
Seaward Dr. TA6: B'wtr 5F 9
Sedge Cl. TA6: B'wtr 3F 13
Sedgemoor Rd. TA6: B'wtr 2A 14
　TA7: Wlvgtn 5H 5
Sedgemoor Splash 6F 9
　(Swimming Pool)
Sedgemoor Way
　TA7: Wlvgtn 5G 5
Sedgemount Ind. Est.
　TA6: B'wtr 2H 9
Selworthy Cl. TA6: B'wtr 4F 13
Selworthy Rd. TA2: Taun 2D 22
Semington Cl. TA1: Taun 1F 29
Severn Cl. TA6: B'wtr 4B 10
Severn Dr. TA1: Taun 1E 29
Seville Ct. TA1: Taun 2H 27
Seymour Rd. TA6: B'wtr 6B 10
Seymour St. TA21: Well 3C 30
Shakespeare Av.
　TA1: Taun 1D 28
Sharman Ct. TA6: B'wtr 5F 9
　(off Waverley Wharf)
Shaulders, The TA2: Taun 3E 23
Shearwater Cl. TA6: B'wtr 2B 14
Sheldon Cl. TA1: Taun 6A 22
Shelley Gro. TA1: Taun 1D 28
Shellthorn Gro. TA6: B'wtr 3F 13
Shepherds Cl. TA6: Wemb 5D 8
Shepherd's Hay TA1: Taun 2G 27
Sheppy's Cider Farm Cen. 5A 26
Sherford 3E 28
Sherford Rd. TA1: Taun 3A 28
Sherford Ter. TA1: Taun 3A 28
Sheridan Cl. TA6: B'wtr 2B 14
Shervage Ct. TA1: Taun 6A 10
Shoe La. TA7: E Bwr 4C 10
Shoreditch 5E 29
Shoreditch Rd. TA1: Taun 3D 28
　TA3: Shore 2F 29
Shovel La. TA6: N Peth 3D 16
Shovel Rd. TA6: N Peth 3C 16
Showell Pk. TA2: Staple 3F 21
Showground Bus. Pk., The
　TA6: B'wtr 4H 13
Showground Rd.
　TA6: B'wtr 4H 13
Shuteleigh TA21: Well 4E 31
Shutemead TA1: Bish H 6E 21
Shutewater Cl.
　TA1: Bish H 6E 21
Shutewater Hill
　TA1: Bish H 6E 21
Shuttern TA1: Taun 1A 28
Sidbrook 1G 23
Silk Mills La.
　TA2: Staple, Taun 3F 21
Silk Mills Rd.
　TA1: Bish H, R'moor 4F 21
Silverdale Cl. TA6: Wemb 6C 8
Silver St. TA1: Taun 1C 28
　TA6: B'wtr 1F 13
Six Acres Cl. TA1: Taun 5E 23
Skimmerton La.
　TA5: Durl, Wemb 6A 8
Slape Cross 5D 10
Slapes Cl. TA2: Taun 1C 22
Small Industries Est., The
　TA4: D'wear 4B 14
Smithy TA1: Bish H 6F 21
Snathe Lea TA4: Bish L 3C 18
Snedden Gro. TA1: Taun 5D 22
Snowbery Ct. TA1: Taun 2E 29
　(off Warwick Gdns.)
Sogg Drove TA7: W'land 3H 15

Somerset Av. TA1: Taun 2F 27
Somerset Bridge 3A 14
Somerset Bri. TA6: B'wtr 3A 14
Somerset County Mus. 6B 22
Somerset Cricket Mus. 6C 22
Somerset Gdns.
　TA6: B'wtr 2A 14
Somerset Pl. TA1: Taun 6C 22
Somerset Rd. TA6: B'wtr 3A 14
Somerset Vw. Cvn. Pk.
　TA6: N Peth 5D 16
Somerton Cl. TA6: B'wtr 1B 14
Somerville Way TA6: B'wtr 2B 14
Sorrento M. TA6: Wemb 4E 9
Southampton Row
　TA2: Taun 2C 22
Southbourne Ho.
　TA6: B'wtr 1E 13
　(off West St.)
Southbrook TA5: Cann 2G 7
Southbrook Cl. TA5: Cann 2G 7
Southfield Cl. TA2: Taun 2C 22
　TA7: Wlvgtn 5H 5
Southgate Av. TA6: B'wtr 2G 13
Southleigh Rd. TA1: Taun 1D 28
Sth. Moor Drove
　TA7: W'land 5G 15
South Rd. TA1: Taun 1C 28
South St. TA1: Taun 1C 28
　TA21: Well 3D 30
South Vw. TA7: P'ton 2G 11
Southview Cl. TA7: W'land 2G 15
Southview Rd. TA7: W'land 2G 15
South Vs. TA4: Cotf L 6B 18
Southwell TA3: Trull 5G 27
Southwood Cl. TA3: Trull 5G 27
Southwood Gro. TA1: Taun 2G 27
Sovereign Rd. TA6: B'wtr 4B 10
Spanish Hill TA7: N New 6E 17
　(in two parts)
Spaxton 1A 12
Spaxton Rd. TA5: B'wtr, Durl 6G 7
　TA6: B'wtr 1A 12
Spearcey Cl. TA3: Trull 6G 27
Spearcey La. TA3: Trull 6G 27
Speke Cl. TA2: Taun 4F 21
Spencer Av. TA2: Taun 4A 22
Spencer Cl. TA6: B'wtr 3E 13
Spillers Cl. TA6: B'wtr 3E 13
Spinneyfield TA4: Bish L 4C 18
Spinney, The TA1: Taun 2H 27
Spoonbill Rd. TA6: B'wtr 1H 13
Springfield Av. TA6: B'wtr 2C 12
Springfield Rd. TA21: Well 2C 30
Springlev Rd. TA6: B'wtr 5B 10
Spring Ri. TA7: P'ton 4C 4
Squares Rd. TA5: Chil T 2F 9
Square, The TA1: Taun 2E 29
　TA7: Wlvgtn 3H 5
Squibbs Cl. TA6: B'wtr 5B 10
Squibbs Ho. TA6: B'wtr 6E 9
Squirrel Ct. TA21: Well 4D 30
Stafford Rd. TA6: B'wtr 2A 14
Stallards TA21: Well 6C 30
Standards Rd. TA7: W'land 5H 15
Standfast Pl. TA2: Taun 2D 22
Standle 6C 30
Stanley Cl. TA2: Taun 4G 21
Stanway Cl. TA2: Taun 3H 21
Staplegrove 3G 21
Staplegrove Mnr.
　TA2: Staple 2H 21
Staplegrove Rd. TA1: Taun 3F 21
　TA2: Staple, Taun 3F 21
Staplehay 6G 27
Statham Cl. TA1: Taun 2G 27
Statham Gro. TA1: Taun 2G 27
Station App. TA1: Taun 5B 22
Station Rd. TA1: Taun 5B 22
　TA2: Nort F 4C 20
　TA4: Bish L 3A 18
　(in two parts)
　TA6: D'ball 5A 4
　TA21: Well 2C 30
Steam Packet Ter.
　TA6: B'wtr 1H 13
　(off All Saints' Ter.)

Steart La. TA3: H'lade 6C 24
Stearts Cotts. TA3: H'lade 6B 24
Stedhams Cl. TA21: Well 2D 30
Stembridge Way TA2: Nort F 4C 20
Stephen St. TA1: Taun 6C 22
Stephen Way TA1: Taun 6C 22
Stepswater Cl. TA1: Taun 6H 21
Stockmoor Cl. TA6: B'wtr 3G 13
Stoford La. TA7: W Buck 6A 26
Stoke La. TA3: Stoke M 4F 29
Stoke Rd. TA1: Taun 3D 28
　TA3: Stoke M 4E 29
Stone Cl. TA1: Taun 4G 27
Stone Drove TA7: B'drip 2G 11
Stonegallows TA1: Taun 2D 26
Stoneleigh TA21: Tone 1B 30
Stoneleigh Cl. TA2: Staple 2G 21
Stoneleigh Cl. TA1: Taun 3G 27
Stoney Furlong TA2: Taun 2D 22
Stoney La. TA4: Bish L 2B 18
Stowey Rd. TA2: Taun 2A 22
Straight Drove TA5: Chil T 1F 9
　TA7: W'land 1H 15
Stratton Cl. TA6: B'wtr 2B 14
Stutts End TA4: Cotf L 6A 18
Suffolk Cl. TA6: B'wtr 2A 14
Suffolk Ct. TA1: Taun 3G 27
　(off Wiltshire Cl.)
Suffolk Cres. TA1: Taun 3G 27
Sully Cl. TA6: B'wtr 5B 10
Summerfield Cl.
　TA21: C'ston 2G 31
Summerfield Cl.
　TA7: W'land 2G 15
Summerfield Ct. TA1: Taun 6A 22
　(off French Weir Cl.)
Summerfield Way
　TA21: C'ston 2H 31
Summerleaze Cres.
　TA2: Taun 2E 23
Summerway Drove
　TA7: E Bwr 1C 14
Sundew La. TA1: Taun 3E 29
Sunnybank Rd. TA6: B'wtr 3E 13
Sunnybrow Cl. TA6: N Peth 2E 17
Sunnymead TA6: B'wtr 3E 13
Sussex Av. TA6: B'wtr 2H 13
Sussex Cl. TA6: B'wtr 2H 13
Sutherland Cl. TA1: Taun 3G 27
Sutherland St. TA1: Taun 3G 27
Swains TA21: Well 5D 30
Swains La. TA21: Well 4D 30
Sweethay 6A 6
Sweethay Cl. TA3: Trull 6G 27
Sweethay La. TA3: Trull 6E 27
Swift Cvn. Pk. TA7: Coss 5H 5
Swingbridge TA6: B'pool 4G 23
Sycamore Cl. TA1: Taun 3E 29
　TA6: B'wtr 6B 10
　TA7: W'land 5H 15
Sycamore Wlk.
　TA3: Creech M 5C 24
Sydenham 5H 9
Sydenham Cl. TA6: B'wtr 5A 10
Sydenham Rd. TA6: B'wtr 5A 10
Sylvan Rd. TA21: Well 3E 31
Sylvan Rd. Trad. Est.
　TA21: Well 3E 31
Sylvan Way TA2: Monk H 2G 23
Symons Way TA6: B'wtr 5G 9

T

Tahnee Ct. TA7: P'ton 3C 4
Tamar Av. TA1: Taun 3D 28
Tancred St. TA1: Taun 6C 22
Tangier 6A 22
Tangier TA1: Taun 6A 22
Tappers La. TA6: N Peth 3D 16
Tapps La. TA7: Wlvgtn 3H 5
Tatham Ct. TA1: Taun 6H 21
Tauntfield Cl. TA1: Taun 1C 28
Taunton 1B 28
Taunton Station 5B 22
Taunton Bus. & Leisure Pk.
　TA1: Taun 5G 23
Taunton Racecourse 6E 29
Taunton Retail Pk.
　TA1: Taun 5G 23

Taunton Rd. TA4: Bish L 3B 18
　TA6: B'wtr 1F 13
　TA6: N Peth 6F 13
　(nr. Bridgwater Rd.)
　TA6: N Peth 6D 16
　(nr. Fore St.)
　TA21: C'ston, Well 2E 31
Taunton Vale Cvn. Pk.
　TA2: Monk H 2H 23
Taylor Cl. TA2: Nort F 3D 20
Taylor Ct. TA6: B'wtr 6G 9
Teak Cl. TA6: B'wtr 5B 10
Teal Cl. TA6: B'wtr 1G 13
Teals Acre TA5: Cann 2F 7
Teck Hill TA6: N Peth 5C 16
Teckhill La. TA6: N Peth 6C 16
Temblett Grn. TA6: Wemb 6C 8
Tetton Cl. TA1: Taun 1B 12
Tetton La. TA4: Bish L 1D 18
Thames Dr. TA1: Taun 6F 23
Theaks M. TA1: Taun 6C 22
Thistle Pk. TA6: B'wtr 4H 13
Thomas St. TA2: Taun 4B 22
Thompson Cl. TA6: B'wtr 5B 10
Thornash Cl. TA2: Monk H 2H 23
Thorncombe Ct. TA6: B'wtr 6A 10
　(off Thorncombe Cres.)
Thorncombe Cres.
　TA6: B'wtr 6A 10
Thurlbear Rd. TA3: Thurl 6F 29
Timbercombe Way
　TA6: B'wtr 1B 12
Tithill 5A 18
Tithill La. TA4: Bish L 5A 18
Toll Ho. Rd. TA5: Cann 1F 7
Tone 1B 30
Tonedale 2B 30
Tonedale Mill Complex
　TA21: Tone 2B 30
Tone Dr. TA6: B'wtr 2H 13
Tone Hill TA21: Tone 1B 30
Toneway TA1: Taun 5D 22
Torridge Mead TA1: Taun 6F 23
Tor Vw. TA7: Wlvgtn 4H 5
Tourist Info. Cen. 6F 9
　(Bridgwater)
Tourist Info. Cen. 3D 30
　(Wellington)
Tower La. TA1: Taun 6A 22
Tower St. TA1: Taun 1A 28
Townsend Rd. TA7: W'land 2H 15
Transform Ind. Est.
　TA6: B'wtr 5G 9
Treborough Cl. TA2: Taun 2D 22
Trendle Rd. TA1: Taun 3F 27
Trent Mdw. TA1: Taun 6F 23
Trevett Rd. TA1: Taun 6F 23
Trevor Rd. TA6: B'wtr 4A 10
Trevor Smith Pl. TA1: Taun 1C 28
Triangle, The TA2: Taun 4B 22
Trinity Bus. Cen. TA1: Taun 1C 28
Trinity Cl. TA21: Well 4C 30
Trinity Cl. TA1: Taun 2F 29
　TA6: B'wtr 5F 9
Trinity Rd. TA1: Taun 1D 28
Trinity St. TA1: Taun 1D 28
Trinity Way
　TA6: B'wtr, Wemb 5E 9
Triscombe Av. TA6: B'wtr 1D 12
Triscombe Cl. TA2: Taun 2A 22
Tristram Dr. TA3: Creech M 4C 24
Trull 5G 27
Trull Grn. Dr. TA3: Trull 5G 27
Trull Rd. TA1: Taun 3H 27
Tuckerton La. TA7: N New 6F 17
Tudor Rd. TA6: B'wtr 4G 13
Tulip Tree Rd. TA6: B'wtr 6B 10
Turin Path TA6: Wemb 4E 9
Turner Cl. TA6: B'wtr 1G 13
Turner Rd. TA2: Taun 3A 22
Twyford Pl. TA21: Well 4D 30
Tyne Pk. TA1: Taun 1F 29
Tynte Rd. TA6: B'wtr 6B 10

U

Union Ga. TA1: Taun 6D 22
Union St. TA6: B'wtr 5H 9
　(in two parts)

Upcot Cres. TA1: Taun 2F 27
Upcott 6D 20
Upcott Rd. TA4: Bish H 6C 20
Up. High St. TA1: Taun 1B 28
Up. Holway Rd. TA1: Taun 2E 29

V

Valetta Pl. TA6: B'wtr 6F 9
Valley Rd. TA1: Taun 5E 23
Venn Cl. TA4: Cotf L 6A 18
          (in two parts)
Venture Eleven, The
   TA2: Taun 4D 22
Venture Way TA2: Taun 3E 23
Vera St. TA2: Taun 3B 22
Verona Ct. TA6: Wemb 4E 9
Verriers TA6: N Peth 2D 16
Vicarage Cl.
   TA3: Creech M................5C 24
   TA7: W'land..................2G 15
Vicarage La.
   TA3: Creech M................5C 24
Vicarage Lawns
   TA3: Creech M................4C 24
Vicarage Rd. TA7: Wlvgtn......4H 5
Vicars La. TA6: Wemb 6D 8
Vickery Cl. TA6: B'wtr 2D 12
Victoria Ga. TA1: Taun 6D 22
Victoria Parkway
   TA1: Taun 5D 22
Victoria Rd. TA6: B'wtr..........6E 9
Victoria St. TA1: Taun 6D 22
   TA21: Well......................3D 30
Victory Rd. TA2: Taun 3C 22
Vilberie Cl. TA2: Nort F 3D 20
Viney St. TA1: Taun 1D 28
Virginia Orchard
   TA3: Ruish....................6A 24
Viscount Sq. TA6: B'wtr 4E 9
Vivary Ga. TA1: Taun 1B 28
Vivary Heights TA1: Taun 2A 28
Vivary Rd. TA1: Taun 1A 28

W

Wade Cl. TA7: W'land 4H 15
Wadham Cl. TA6: B'wtr..........5B 10
Walkers Ga. TA21: Well 4D 30
Walnut Cl. TA1: Bish H 6F 21
   TA7: P'ton 3C 4
Walnut Dr. TA6: B'wtr..........2A 14
Walpole 3A 4
Walpole Drove TA6: P'lett 2A 4
Walter Barnett Ho.
   TA6: B'wtr......................1E 13
       (off Albert St.)
Walton Cl. TA6: B'wtr 6B 10
Wambrook Cl. TA1: Taun 3A 28
Wansbeck Grn. TA1: Taun 1F 29
Ward La. TA7: C'zoy 5G 11
Wardleworth Way
   TA21: Tone 2C 30
Wares La. TA6: Wemb 5D 8
Warren Cl. TA6: B'wtr 5F 9

Warren St. TA21: R Grn 5B 30
Warres Rd. TA2: Taun............2E 23
Warwick Av. TA6: B'wtr 2A 14
Warwick Gdns. TA1: Taun......2E 29
Warwick Rd. TA2: Taun..........2C 22
Washington Gdns.
   TA6: B'wtr......................6E 9
Wassail Vw. TA2: Nort F 4C 20
Waterfield Cl. TA1: Bish H 1F 27
Waterfield Dr. TA1: Bish H 1E 27
Waterford Cl. TA6: B'wtr........3G 13
Waterleaze TA1: Taun............3E 23
Waterloo TA7: P'ton 3C 4
Waterloo Cl. TA7: P'ton 3C 4
Waterloo Rd. TA21: Well........3C 30
Watermans Mdw.
   TA6: Wemb......................5E 9
Watery La. TA6: N Peth 2D 16
Watsons La. TA6: B'wtr 5E 9
Watts La. TA4: Bish L..........1A 18
Waverley Rd. TA6: B'wtr 5F 9
Waverley Wharf TA6: B'wtr 5F 9
Waverney Cl. TA1: Taun 1F 29
Wayside TA3: Trull................6G 27
Weacombe Rd. TA2: Taun......3B 22
Webbers TA4: Bish L............4C 18
Webbers Cl. TA21: Well 5E 31
Webbers Way TA7: P'ton 4B 4
Wedlands TA2: Taun..............3B 22
Weirfield Grn. TA1: Taun 5H 21
Welland Cl. TA1: Taun 1F 29
Wellesley Cl. TA1: Taun........3G 27
Wellesley Pk. TA21: Well 4E 31
Wellesley St. TA2: Taun 4B 22
Wellesley Theatre, The 4D 30
WELLINGTON & DISTRICT
   COTTAGE HOSPITAL 4D 30
Wellington Mus. 3D 30
Wellington New Rd.
   TA1: Bish H, Taun............1E 27
Wellington Rd. TA1: Taun......1G 27
   TA6: B'wtr......................6H 9
Wellington Sports Cen. 3C 30
Wells Cl. TA2: Taun..............2C 22
Wellsprings 2C 22
Wellsprings Rd. TA2: Taun 3A 22
Wellsprings Sports Cen., The
   ....1B 22
Well, The TA21: R Grn 4B 30
Wembdon 5C 8
Wembdon Ct. TA6: B'wtr 1E 13
Wembdon Hill TA6: Wemb 5B 8
Wembdon Orchard
   TA6: Wemb 5C 8
Wembdon Ri.
   TA6: B'wtr, Wemb 5D 8
Wembdon Rd. TA6: B'wtr 1D 12
Wesley Cl. TA1: Taun............3G 27
Wessex Cl. TA6: B'wtr..........1A 14
Wessex Rd. TA1: Taun 4A 28
W. Approach Rd. TA7: P'ton 3E 5
W. Bower La. TA5: Durl 1A 12
W. Bow Ho. TA6: B'wtr 1E 13
W. Buckland Rd.
   TA21: C'ston, Well 5F 31

Westerkirk Ga. TA2: Staple....3G 21
Western Way TA6: B'wtr........4F 9
W. Field Cl. TA1: Taun 2E 27
Westfield Cl. TA6: B'wtr........1E 13
Westford 4A 30
Westford Cl. TA21: West........4A 30
Westford Ct. TA21: West........4A 30
Westford Dr. TA21: West........4A 30
Westgate St. TA1: Taun 1A 28
Westleigh Rd. TA1: Taun 1D 28
Westmoor Drove
   TA3: N Curry....................5F 25
Westonzoyland 2G 15
Westonzoyland Rd.
   TA6: B'wtr......................1H 13
   TA7: D'wear, W'land........1A 14
Westover Grn. TA6: B'wtr......1E 13
West Quay TA6: B'wtr..........6F 9
Westridge Way
   TA4: Bish L....................4B 18
West St. TA4: Bish L 1A 18
   TA6: B'wtr......................1E 13
West Vw. TA3: Creech M......3C 24
West Vs. TA4: Cotf L 6B 18
Westwood Rd. TA6: B'wtr 4B 10
Wheatleigh Cl. TA1: Taun 2A 28
Wheatley Cres. TA1: Taun 5D 22
Wheatstones TA4: Bish L......3C 18
Whirligig La. TA1: Taun 6B 22
Whitebeam Cl. TA6: B'wtr 4B 10
Whitehall TA1: Taun..............5B 22
White Hart La. TA21: Well 3D 30
Whites Cl. TA6: B'wtr 3E 13
White St. TA3: Creech M......6E 25
Whitfield Rd. TA6: B'wtr........4B 10
Whiting La. TA6: N Peth 3D 16
Whitmore La. TA2: Staple......1H 21
Whitmore Rd. TA2: Taun 2A 22
Wild Oak La. TA3: Trull........5H 27
Wilfred Rd. TA1: Taun 6C 22
Wilkins Rd. TA6: B'wtr..........6B 10
William St. TA2: Taun............4B 22
Willie Gill Ct. TA1: Taun 6A 22
      (off Wood St.)
Willocks Cl. TA21: Well 4D 30
Willoughby Rd. TA6: B'wtr 1C 12
Willow Cl. TA1: Taun 3F 29
   TA7: W'land....................5H 15
Willow Ct. TA6: B'wtr............6B 10
Willow Grn. TA7: C'zoy..........5F 11
Willow Wlk. TA6: B'wtr 1A 14
Wills Ind. Est. TA6: B'wtr......1G 13
Wills Rd. TA6: B'wtr..............4E 13
Wilton 2B 28
Wilton Cl. TA1: Taun 1A 28
Wilton Gro. TA1: Taun 1A 28
Wilton Lands TA1: Taun 2B 28
Wilton Orchard TA1: Taun 2A 28
Wilton St. TA1: Taun 1A 28
Wiltshire Cl. TA1: Taun 2G 27
Wiltshire Ct. TA1: Taun 2G 27
      (off Wiltshire Cl.)
Wimborne Cl. TA1: Taun 1F 29
Winchester St. TA1: Taun 6C 22
Winckworth Way
   TA1: Taun 5C 22

Wind Down Cl. TA6: B'wtr 1B 12
Windmill Cres.
   TA7: Wlvgtn......................5H 5
Windsor Cl. TA1: Taun 3G 27
Windsor Dr. TA6: B'wtr 4B 10
      (off Whitfield Rd.)
Windsor Rd. TA6: B'wtr 4A 10
Winsbeer La. TA21: West 2A 30
Winslade Cl. TA2: Taun 3D 22
Winston Cl. TA2: Taun 4A 22
Winters Orchard
   TA3: Stoke M..................5H 29
Wireworks Est., The
   TA6: B'wtr......................2H 9
Witches Wlk. TA6: B'wtr 3E 13
Witham Cl. TA1: Taun 1F 29
Withiel Dr. TA5: Cann 2D 6
Withy Gro. Cl. TA6: B'wtr......4B 10
Wolmer Cl. TA6: B'wtr..........3E 13
Woodbury Rd. TA6: B'wtr 1D 12
Woodland Av. TA7: W'land....2G 15
Woodland Rd. TA2: Taun 3E 23
Woodlands Dr. TA3: Ruish 6A 24
Woodridge Mead
   TA4: Bish L....................3C 18
Woodrush Cl. TA1: Taun 3E 29
Woodstock Rd. TA1: Taun 5A 22
Wood St. TA1: Taun 6A 22
Woolavington 4H 5
Woolavington Hill
   TA7: B'drip, Wlvgtn..........6H 5
Woolavington Right Drove
   TA7: C'zoy 3E 15
Woolavington Rd.
   TA7: P'ton, Wlvgtn..........4C 4
Woolmersdon 1C 16
Wordsworth Av. TA6: B'wtr....5E 9
Wordsworth Dr. TA1: Taun 6D 22
Worthy La. TA3: Creech M 3D 24
Wren Cl. TA1: Bish H 6G 21
Wrenmoor Cl. TA6: B'wtr 2A 14
Wyatts Fld. TA3: Trull 5G 27
Wye Av. TA6: B'wtr 1A 14
Wylds Rd. TA6: B'wtr............4G 9
Wyndham Rd. TA2: Taun 3A 22
   TA6: B'wtr......................5A 10
Wyvern Rd. TA1: Taun..........4A 28

Y

Yallands Hill
   TA2: Monk H....................2G 23
Yarde Pl. TA1: Taun..............6A 22
Yarford 2H 19
Yarlington Cl. TA2: Nort F 4E 21
Yeo La. TA6: B'wtr 3H 13
Yeo Rd. TA6: B'wtr 3H 13
Yew Tree La. TA2: B'pool 4G 23
Yonder Mead TA4: Bish L......4C 18
York Rd. TA1: Taun 5E 23
   TA6: B'wtr......................3F 13

Z

Zeta Cl. TA7: H'sey................3C 10